The Custom Road Bike

Guy Andrews

Laurence King Publishing

LAURENCE KING

First published in Great Britain in 2010
This paperback edition first published in 2012 by
Laurence King Publishing Ltd
361–373 City Road
London EC1V 1LR
United Kingdom

T: 020 7841 6900
F: 020 7841 6910
e-mail: enquiries@laurenceking.com
www.laurenceking.com

A catalogue for this book is available from the British Library.

ISBN: 978 1 85669 813 9

Design: Jonathan Bacon
Photography: unless otherwise credited, all photography by Gerard Brown

Printed and bound in China

Contents

I've started this book many times, usually in daydreams, on training rides in the hills or driving home from a race. So, like you, I have probably spent longer than is healthy thinking about bikes. The inspiration for this book, however, all goes back to a small cupboard that was in my bedroom when I first began bike racing over 25 years ago. This was where I kept all my new bike parts, all in boxes and ready for building the next race bike I was saving up for.

However 'bad' I have it now, it's difficult to remember my enthusiasm when I first ventured into a 'lightweight' cycle dealer and gazed into a cabinet full of Italian components. My many questions often meant long discussions with the mechanics. I made mistakes, broke and bodged things and experimented with all sorts of variations of bicycle set-up. The beauty of the bicycle is not only in its form and function, but also, as I found, in its component parts and its assembly.

Nowadays, as a magazine editor, I'm very fortunate to be able to indulge my passion for bikes every day. I also get to talk to a lot of very talented people who are involved in bicycle design and technology and who all have one thing in common – they love what they do.

The time that you spend planning a new bike is considerable, and is perhaps the best part of the process. It's still what wakes me up in the middle of the night with solutions to component problems and plans for the next bike – they are always a work in progress.

This book may be about your next bike, or perhaps it will help you to upgrade a bike you already have. It will be a companion when making decisions about your bike, not a guide to everything and anything to do with bikes. It is concerned only with performance bikes, and road bikes at that. Track and time trial bikes do come into it and so does that most awkward of road-bike brothers, the cyclo-cross bike. These are the bikes that I know most about, so they are all here.

Each chapter covers a specific element of the bike, with add-on features about the largest subject area – frame builders. I've built countless bikes, but never a frame, so I've picked these people to share their experiences. They explore the diverse nature of design and manufacturing at the sharp end. Unlike mainstream bike companies (which design and market mass-produced bikes or 'units'), these companies work on high-quality products, most of which are used by professional teams, Tour de France riders and you, the discerning enthusiast.

Bikes are like music, with many genres and many styles. What overwhelms me about them is the breadth of different approaches and diverse opinions. It's no surprise that these sometimes cross-pollinate and influence each other – something that is evident with many of the builders I have spoken to. Bike builders care about what they create and they want you to get more from your bike and more fun from your riding. They are all passionate about that.

And, as Eddy Merckx famously said, 'Life without passion is so empty'.

Bikes

The Best Bike for You

What is the best road bike you can buy? I am asked this all the time and the answer is never simple. So my initial response may often be, 'How much have you got to spend?', usually followed by a lot of more important and searching questions. It's not all about money, though, it's a consultation process that can last hours, even days. So, when considering your options, always mull over the following points:

What kind of rider are you? You could be a strong racer, an enthusiastic newcomer who is looking to improve or perhaps the gentle tourist type who just wants a lovely bike for long rides in the summer sun. **What style of riding will you be doing?** The demands that racing, training, sportive or 'just for fun' rides place on a bike are all very specific. If you will want to upgrade and start racing you may need a different bike. **Are you a heavy rider or are you heavy on equipment? Will you look after your bike?** If you don't keep your bike clean and if you tend to trash wheels and components, you may be using the wrong kit.

There are no wrong answers to these questions, but the answers are important. A road bike for riding the mountains fast is completely different to a bike for riding the mountains and admiring the view. And the answers to these questions are particular to you, so they are where you should start your search for the ideal bike. Don't think that it's all about what road bike the professional riders ride either – they are highly trained athletes and their bikes are particular to them, often custom made and, for that reason, invariably totally inappropriate to lesser mortals. We are not lining up for the Tour de France, after all. There are very few bikes in this book that will be ridden by Tour de France professionals; the builders and manufacturers consulted here are all interested in the artisan approach rather than the pure performance end of the market.

There are many things to factor in to a racing bike, but it is always worth remembering that a race-pedigree bike straight from the professional peloton will rarely be the right fit and the right size for you. If you are very tall or have injury issues that require a frame builder's specific attention, it's unlikely that a pro replica bike will suit your specific needs.

So, after considering the purpose of the bike you are about to buy, think about what it is you want to achieve from your cycling. Try to keep these reasons ahead of any personal paint preferences or what bike so-and-so is riding this year. Pro riders are a pretty pragmatic bunch – they give their bikes back at the end of each season (and swing a leg over the next one that comes their way), but your bike is going to be with you for a little longer. There is no point riding the lightest, highest-tech race machine that money can buy if you can't get further than the corner shop, or collapse with backache before you reach 50k (30 miles) – with this purchase, comfort should always be the top priority.

So, in my opinion, the best bike for you is the one that you want to ride every day and the one that says something to you. This means that you should pay close attention to how it was built, who built it and how well it fits. There are many people who understand this process and some of the finest exponents are featured in these pages. Feed them with the right information about your riding and I am certain that they will provide you with your best bike.

The Road Bike

The standard road bike design is the basis for all bicycles, and the one from which they all take their design cues, whether track pursuit bike or mountain bike. The bikes used by a professional racer may change slightly from race to race, and those used to win the Paris–Roubaix, a World Road Race title or even the prologue of the Tour de France will have different requirements, but they are all very similar in their structure and design. Road racing bikes are multiple geared and usually have dropped or hooked handlebars, which will allow for multiple road-riding positions: 'on the tops', with your hands on the top section of the bars for cruising and climbing big mountains; 'on the hoods', for faster speeds and bunch riding, with your hands always in touch with the brake and gear controls; and 'on the drops', for flat-out speed and a more aerodynamic position.

For over a century the standard road racing bike has had a double diamond pattern frame (see *Frame Geometry*, page 42). However, tweaks to the fundamental geometry have been very limited, mainly because the design is the best combination of lightness, rider fit and application to the job. Some would argue that the UCI (Union Cycliste Inernationale), which now legislates on competition bicycle specification (weight, tube specification and geometry), has kept it this way, and others would also say that there may be a number of instances when this design could be bettered, but these are often compromised in the reality of belting up the Alpe d'Huez. You can't go very fast across cobblestones on a recumbent HPV and you can't race cyclo-cross on a BMX.

The road component group that adorns a road bike is also a standard that has been around for a long time. Of course things have developed to make it a better functioning machine, but the chain drive and derailleur-geared approach has been the same for decades – because it works and is easy to service and maintain.

Materials have changed the nature of the modern road racing chassis. The most recent of these, carbon fibre, has given designers a freedom in tube shapes and design that had previously been impossible. The resulting bicycle is arguably lighter, stiffer and more responsive than ever, but carbon can cause problems when poorly constructed and designed. This reinforces the reason why the road-bike makers featured in this book are a breed apart. They all produce well-made examples of the standard road racing bike, with the added benefit that they can engineer a bike specially for you, with the basic design of the frame tweaked according to your skill and preferred riding style.

'Materials have changed the nature of the modern road racing chassis. The most recent of these, carbon fibre, has given designers a freedom in tube shapes and design that had previously been impossible.'

The Time Trial Bike

There are a lot of misconceptions about what makes a good time trial bike. A fast time trial will combine a comfortable, powerful and relaxed position with a fluid, consistent pedalling technique. Before you even consider aerodynamics think about how well the bike will fit you, consult a fitting expert and study your position very carefully. One of the basic fit mistakes is that riders think that the saddle should be higher than on a standard road bike, because a higher saddle position is going to be more powerful. But, when combined with a lower handlebar height (because logically, this should help you cut into the air more) you will tip your hips and throw your body further forward, with the result that you will lose power. I even see professional riders making this mistake and, although their road position may be spot-on, they look totally at sea when racing against the clock. I'm sure that many would go faster on a standard road bike with time trial bars.

The fit is all important, so consider this before having an expensive time trial rig built up, especially one such as those intended for professional team riders' use – they are highly trained and flexible athletes so they can cope with extremes of position, even if they do sometimes get it wrong. The time trial bikes that professional teams use simply don't fit everyone and can create several problems when they are made generally available to everyone. Fit is far more important than aerodynamics – I once rode Chris Boardman's Lotus pursuit bike, and it nearly put me in hospital because his super-aero tuck position was so extreme that I nearly slipped a disc. The drop between the saddle and the bars was so big it was nigh-on impossible to ride for even the most flexible rider, but for him it was really aerodynamic and, more significantly, comfortable. As a pursuit rider he was unique, with a physiology that could cope with the demands the bike made on his body.

However, aerodynamics is important in time trialling and this is a big topic. Proven advantages in clothing, aero helmets, wheels and the triathlon-influenced handlebar position have

made the 'race of truth' rather complicated. Specialist aero equipment is big business and the popularity of triathlon has helped many companies grow their ranges. Since Greg Lemond used his Scott bar extensions with armrests to win the 1989 Tour de France it has standardized TT bikes. However, the UCI have made some big changes to what is legal for racing, and this often means that the manufacturers will usually produce only components that comply with the regulations. Always bear in mind that the bars and stem need to be in the perfect position rather than made from the perfect materials. Gear shifting and brake levers have also had the aero treatment, with the gear levers positioned on the bar ends and the brake levers pared down to the thinnest possible aero section.

Wheels and tyres may make you faster, so spending more money on these will make more sense than having the best brakes and gears. Aerodynamics is far more important if you are travelling at higher speeds and in varying wind and surface conditions, so a wheel for the track pursuit will differ from the wheel you use for a long hilly time trial on the road in high crosswinds. A rear disc wheel and a deep-section front wheel is the standard time trial set-up, allowing for stability and aerodynamics (a disc front wheel is almost impossible to steer in a cross wind). Wheels are a separate subject, and are dealt with later (see Wheels, page 72).

The Track Bike

It needs careful sizing and accurate building to achieve the perfect handling and precise control that you'll need at speeds up to 60kph (37mph) (if you are Chris Hoy) but whatever speed you race at, a track bike has to be very different from its roadgoing cousin.

A single fixed gear will seem strange to road riders at first, but it makes perfect sense on the track. You quickly learn the subtle skill of easing off to brake and the single ratio soon becomes second nature. Gears for bicycles are traditionally measured in inches and this tradition is still the peculiar language of track specialists, who will talk of using a '90', or an '86', which makes little sense if you are used to 20-speed road bike gear ratios. This seemingly arbitrary number refers to the distance the bike will travel with one revolution of the pedals. What size you use depends on your required cadence (speed of pedalling), but the basic gears used

'Perhaps the purest bicycle ever conceived, the track bike has nothing added, no gears and no brakes. That said, its specialized technical requirements have to cope with the demands of racing on a steeply banked track at high speeds.'

are 49 x 15 or 50 x 15, depending on the event and the nature of the track. It's not that surprising that track riders develop a high cadence and a fluid pedalling style as they can't change into a higher gear to sprint or a lower one if they are suffering in an endurance event. Special cranks are used on the track – they have a perfectly positioned single chainwheel for the ideal chainline between sprocket and drive. Track bikes usually have shorter arms than those used on a road bike – 165mm cranks arms are usually preferred, as they accelerate quickly and allow for pedal clearance from the steep banks on the corners of the velodrome.

Steering on the track becomes an even more subtle art than it is on the road, as slight changes to body position can change direction dramatically. Just watch a kilo rider at full speed and you will see that his arms remain seemingly static, fixed yet relaxed, with the bike rarely moving from the desired fastest line around the track. But see the same rider sprinting and, while he may look the same at speed, a skilled exponent can alter position on the track with the smallest of flicks on the bars. The fork geometry of the track bike allows for this as it has a much more precise feel for quick changes in direction. While a road fork may have a gentle rake to add comfort and slow steering control, comfort on a track bike is largely irrelevant, so fast, twitchy, almost straight forks are used. The result is a direct feeling bike, really suited only to riding the velodrome, and certainly not intended for city traffic.

Wheels and tyres for track racing are usually of the tubular variety as they can be made very light in weight and they can also be ridden (albeit carefully) when punctured. Wheel choice will depend on the event, with disc wheels and aero section rims favoured for speed, added stiffness and cheating the wind. Elsewhere on the track bike the handlebar set-up also has a slightly different approach from that of the road bike, with deeper drops often preferred for a lower, more powerful position, and pedals sometimes swapped for those with more secure fastening. These are the basics – the rest is down to specifics for the individual events.

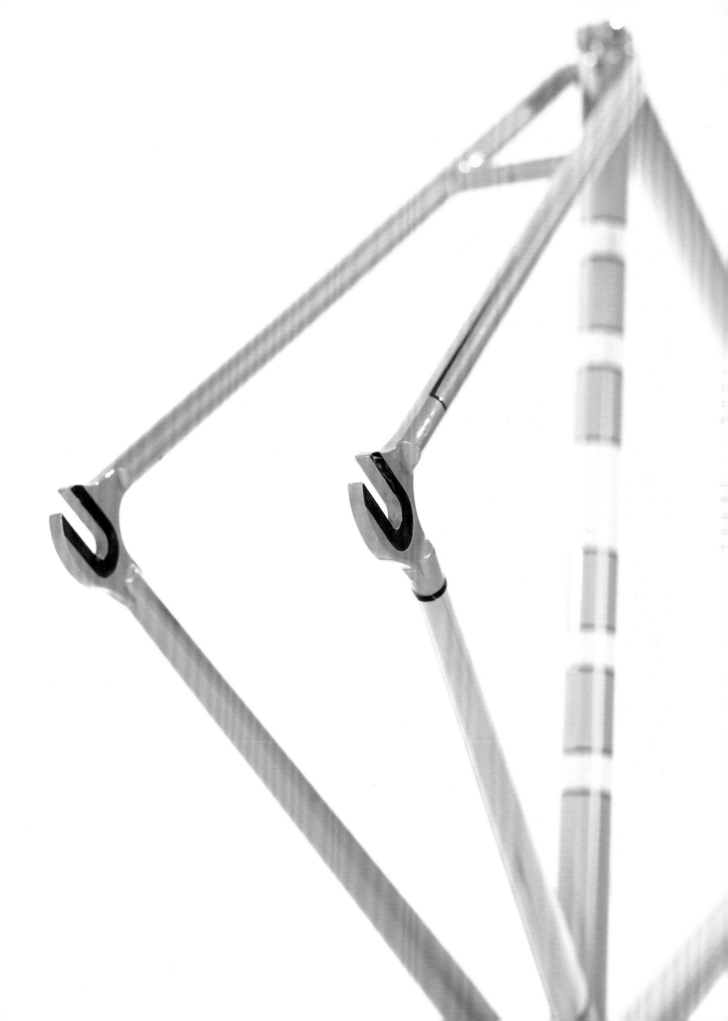

The Cyclo-cross Bike

Cyclo-cross is an odd sport, developing as a winter pastime blending the all-out speed of road cycling with the technical skill of mountain biking on terrain not exactly suited to pure road bike design. So it needs a bike that has significant frame and equipment differences, while being closely associated with those of a road machine.

In the early days of cyclo-cross, a second-hand touring or training frame and cast-off racing gears were cobbled together to make a suitable racing bike. Nothing really matched, and nothing really worked that well either. In the 1980s, kit grew more specialized and aluminium became sought after as a frame material. Aluminium bikes weighed quite a few pounds less than most steel cyclo-cross bikes of the time. The exponents of these lightweight frames were Italian frame manufacturers Alan and French manufacturers Vitus.

For the past ten years the increasing popularity of cyclo-cross has meant that it is a significant niche in the bicycle industry and the new equipment that has been developed has helped redefine the sport. Better tyres have followed better frames and now even the brakes are almost usable. Super lightweight and durable full carbon exotica powers the professional European cyclo-cross peloton, and manufacturers are keen to have at least an entry level cyclo-cross bike in their range. The American companies especially have embraced the 'new' sport, and they have had a valuable influence, stemming directly from the development of the mountain bike, applying the latest technology to the oldest off-road sport. Although the UCI stepped in to put a stop to any useful advances (most notably disc brakes), and although it's frustrating for designers, it brings us back again to that level playing field. Mountain biking managed to introduce better, lighter and stronger component parts that have since drifted through to the road-bike market too, so performance cyclo-cross bikes are now much safer and totally suited to the rutted tracks and tough muddy courses that define the sport.

Generally speaking cyclo-cross requires a bike with a slacker seat and head angle, a higher bottom bracket and a longer wheelbase, so custom-built cyclo-cross frames are often the best route to the right size. As they are all designed with comfort and stability in mind, a shorter top tube and higher handlebar position may also be a good idea. Frame size will usually be smaller than the bike you use on the road, and most manufacturers have allowed for this in their 'off-the-peg' geometries. The higher bottom bracket in the design is intended to allow for greater obstacle clearance (for hopping over logs or hurdles without fouling the chainrings). This can often mean that the frame appears slightly smaller than a standard road frame as it has to allow for a greater stand-over height. Added to all this, the frame has to have more tyre clearance than a standard road frame. Hence there is a longer wheelbase, which also has a useful stabilizing effect on the handling.

Bigger tyres and the trail debris that gets stuck to them need plenty of space to rotate. This is also the main reason why cantilever brakes are preferred over the standard side-pull road design, which, aside from the tyres and the frame geometry, is the only major difference between a cyclo-cross racing bike and its on-road counterpart.

Other more subtle differences are in the gearing and component elements of the cyclo-cross bike. Many opt for pretty low gearing with a 46- or 48-tooth outer ring and a 38-tooth inner ring matched to a 12–26 or even a 12–28 rear cassette, while some will use just one ring with chain guards to prevent unshipping the chain. These choices will depend on the technicality of the course and the rider's fitness and preferred pedalling cadence. Seat posts, handlebars, pedals and stems were, until recent times, just not up to the job in cyclo-cross, with bent posts and even broken bars being a regular occurrence. So, in the interests of safety, stick with components that are strong, simple and easy to maintain.

The wheels for cyclo-cross vary depending on the conditions. Deep-section carbon is popular as the wheels roll better through mud and are less likely to sink in. Riders will usually opt for road wheels, often lightweight ones, as any weight saved on the bike helps with run-ups and when carrying the bike. On the wheels are usually cyclo-cross tubulars. Although decent clincher tyres for cyclo-cross are now readily available, tubs still rule the serious races as they have better puncture resistance and can be run at lower pressures for greater comfort and speed over rough terrain.

CROSS C50

COL

Ben Serotta

41 Geyser Road
Saratoga Springs
NY 12866
USA
www.serotta.com
+1 518 584 1221

It is something of an irony that one of the godfathers of custom frame-building has a completely different philosophy from the rest of the bespoke bicycle industry. Being almost devoid of sentimentality Ben Serotta, by his own admission, is indifferent to anything that smells vaguely retro – hence the major divergence between Serotta bikes and the majority of art-house custom builders. For him, craftsmanship and build integrity are necessary but never solely sufficient qualities.

Ben Serotta has absolutely no interest in doing the same thing this year as he did last year – what drives him forward with a scientist's head and artist's heart is the idea of constantly improving bicycle design. So, in that sense, Serotta is perhaps the living embodiment of anti-retro, and it is Ben's restless engineer's quest for progression and forward movement that has kept Serotta Competition Cycles at the forefront of bicycle design and technology for almost four decades.

Serotta control all their tubing manufacturing processes, from raw material through to finished products. It is remarkable that such a small company could take raw titanium and carbon in through the back door and wheel beautiful handmade bicycles out the front door – even the intricate dropouts and small machined parts are CNCd in-house at Saratoga.

Everything for Ben and his co-workers at Saratoga Springs has been in pursuit of one thing – performance. It drives the entire company from the torch down. Serotta's other obsessions have always been bike-fitting and cycling biomechanics, and the Serotta School of Cycling Ergonomics has been almost solely responsible for driving standards and awareness of fitting throughout the cycling world.

'I love my steel bikes. We evolved much of our design concept in steel. But it is not the best material simply because, sooner or later, more likely than not, corrosion will compromise the material and weaken it. '

Materials used:
Carbon fibre, titanium, steel, aluminium (some fittings) and steel.

Employees:
32

Price range:
US$3,000–10,000 – custom frame and fork.

Waiting period (average!):
6–8 weeks.

Frames built per year (average):
2,500

Who are your customers and how would you 'define' them?
People who are passionate about cycling.

How long have you been building bikes?
Since 1972.

What started your interest in bicycle engineering/design?
In a broad sense, there was never a clear beginning. As a kid, I was happier taking things apart, figuring out how they worked and dreaming of ways to make whatever it was better – more functional, more aesthetically pleasing, simplified etc…so design is just in my DNA. In 1974 I started reshaping tubes to improve lateral stiffness or aerodynamics. In 1985 I stepped up efforts to maximize material potential, developing the Colorado Concept tube platform.

I guess I can say that there are two motivating forces behind our product design and obsession with innovation; 1) as mentioned previously, it's just a part of me, passed on from previous generations; and 2) we are a company based on the principle that we have to continually justify our existence. What I mean by that is that for as long as I've been in the bicycle business there has never been a shortage of nice bicycles. Builders from the US, UK, France, Italy and Japan have provided plenty of choice for elegantly crafted bicycles…so why add to the list? I'm a 1960s idealist at heart. I'm driven to make a difference and since I didn't have the patience for academia (at one time I'd intended to be an environmental biologist) I've committed my company to continually challenge itself to deliver real innovation, not just foofoo fluffy stuff, but concepts that enhance the cycling experience.

Who taught you to build?
Although she's never built a bicycle, I have to give my mother the most credit. In a lot of ways she has been my principal mentor, less by teaching than by example, more in her attitude and approach than in method – my wiring comes from her…it's a 'How am I going to do this?' approach rather than 'Why can't I do this?' Closer to bicycles, she showed me how to light her jeweller's torch, spent an hour or so with me and walked away. In 1972 I was able to spend a few months working at the Witcomb Lightweights atelier in Deptford SE8 (just months ahead of Richard Sachs and Peter Weigle). I'd say that I more observed there than learned. It was very primitive, both in rustic setting and in tooling and method, which, at eighteen, made it in an odd way romantic. But the best builders' work was brilliant and then there were other builders whose work…

*'I am a modest person. Truthfully
I am. But if I didn't truly believe that
we build the best bikes in the world
I would leave the business.'*

The Custom Road Bike

not so much. There were two who I was allowed to 'help'. But it did provide a sense of process and feel for steel. Shortly after my return to the US I visited a guy named Pepi Limongi, a French builder who had moved to the US, and later a father and son team – Cuevas. Cuevas and Limongi both made frames differently from each other and from Witcomb, and they were all fantastic. Realizing that essentially all builders of that time period built differently (but with the same materials) made me feel right at home evolving my own way of doing things.

Who influences what you do now (if not all of the above)?
Everyone and no one.

What is the best material for frame manufacturing (and why)?
It depends. I really struggle with this. I think we make too many models of frames, but that stems from the fact that we use three materials, individually and in combination, and every time I sit down to trim our line I get stuck because each material has its own unique flavour. I like all the bikes we build. To me, it's important that each model can stand firmly on its own validity and raison d'être. It's a tough call. All of our bikes are designed and crafted to be really used, ridden hard, built for the real world, so we take safety and longevity seriously, which, in a large part, is why I am so comfortable with the value proposition that all of our bikes have. We don't build with aluminium. It is far and away the worst choice of all modern frame materials, almost matched by magnesium, which we also don't use. They are wonderful materials in certain applications but neither will provide long-term service without considerable risk of failure. Steel is wonderful for a time. I love my steel bikes. We evolved much of our design concept in steel. But it is not the best material simply because, sooner or later, more likely than not, corrosion will compromise the material and weaken it. Rust inhibitors help, alloying helps, but nothing is foolproof. Today, in an effort to compete with a market that craves newer and lighter… many builders are making frames that use materials with such thin walls and/ or with such hard alloys that long-term viability is at serious risk. Materials manufacturers are stretching the reasonable boundaries of process control. As collectibles, they are fine, as long-term cycling partners – not a good idea. So why do we still build with steel? Because as long as a cyclist understands that life expectancy is not limitless, and we avoid fanciful notions of trying to make steel bikes as light as those of titanium or carbon, steel provides a relatively economical way to deliver a phenomenal ride.

Titanium does everything very well and can be manipulated much like steel so that we can have great control over performance – and it's absolutely corrosion proof and durable.

As a designer though carbon fibre offers the limitless potential. I try to explain it like this. Think of crayons. They are sold in sets of 10, 25, 50, 75 and 150 colours. The metals are each like the box of 10, with alloying and diameter range. Add shaping to the metals and you get the box of 25, but with carbon, you're getting the mega box. Of course it's what you do with it that really matters – some companies still use only three colours. We try to see what we can do using more colours, and at this point the potential is pretty overwhelming.

Each material has its advantages and disadvantages. I would not want to choose only one of these two. The good news is that no matter what we do, the ride 'feel' will never be exactly the same. Both can be enjoyed, which shouldn't seem an uncomfortable consideration – a little variety is one of life's pleasures.

How do you size your customers?
We produced the first multi-adjustable 'Serotta Size-Cycle' in 1979 and started the world's first dedicated 'Fit-School' in 1998. Serotta launched SICI (Serotta International Cycling Institute) in 2006 as the umbrella organization to take over the Serotta School duties and also to organize the SICI Symposium as a conduit between the scientific and cycling community. The Serotta School and SICI has influenced a whole generation of bike design and how cyclists now interface with their bikes. There are thousands of cyclists the world over pedalling efficiently and injury-free thanks to these developments – whether they ride a Serotta bike right now or not.

What is the most exciting new development in frame design or tubing technology?
I still see a lot of untapped potential. The materials technology paves the way for design innovation.

What's the most important element to the frame?
The cyclist… the fit and balance of the bike to the cyclist.

What do you want to achieve for your customers?
Cycling bliss. We've done our job when their bike makes them a better cyclist or simply makes them want to ride more.

Who is/was the best frame manufacturer or builder and why?
I am a modest person. Truthfully I am. But if I didn't truly believe that we build the best bikes in the world, I would leave the business. I tell you, without hesitation or shame of immodesty, that, one to one, we are the best. That's a claim that is based in truth and value and worth.

But what is the best bicycle in the world? It's the bike that makes you want to ride more, the one that makes you a better cyclist, the one that speaks to you when you are in another inane, insane, redundant meeting, the one that you'll still be riding fast ten (or 20) years from now, the one that delivers the opportunity for you to achieve your personal best, performance you can count on. The bike that understands, no, defines, why you ride.

OK, now having explained myself, I do have a lot of respect and appreciation for many past and present builders and for different reasons. Ernesto Colnago has inspired generations of bike builders while he has been unreasonably generous to countless aspiring racers, as well as having supported so many pro teams, and he is true to his design principles. Also builders like Limongi, Cuevas, Confenti, Masi, Chris Chance and countless others who have aspired to improve what has already been done and make it better and have taken on risk in doing so. I'm less impressed by builders who make the same beautiful bike year after year… it's nice, so what?

The Frame

Frame Design

'If it looks right, it usually is…' Anon

Many manufacturers will hit you with jargon and marketing about frame design, and some of it even makes some sense, but consider this… The first custom road-racing bike I bought was a perfect fit, and I always rode it with a smile, because every pedal rev was tuned in to my physiology. It was sized by Brian Rourke in Stoke-on-Trent, an ex-professional racer who had a keen eye for size. I noted his recommended dimensions in an old notebook, the height of the saddle, top tube length, stem length, and the height and width of the handlebars. I have been sized several times since then, by top cycling academics, scientists and, even once by a computer, and they all (except the computer, which was miles out) came within a few millimetres of Brian's original specification, which is pretty much what I ride now. I learnt more in the few hours he took to fit me for that frame than I had in previous years spent in the local bike shop or through reading books and magazines. Experience is the key ingredient in an expert fit, and when it comes to frame building I was no expert.

And that is why this chapter is more an introduction to the basic information you need in order to start looking for the right fit. I have discussed many of the issues here with several frame builders and the results are more or less a consensus of their opinions, but (and it's a big but) there have been many bigger books written on this subject – and not so long ago it was so involved that it was a university degree subject. So this chapter explains only the very basic elements of frame design. Everyone is different and there are no shortcuts to the perfect bike. A bicycle's frame is like a car's chassis, as you are like the bicycle's engine.

However, the importance of good fit cannot be over-stressed. A common problem when buying a bike from a dealer is deciding to take what is in stock, perhaps because it's a good deal or even because you like the colour/brand/specification. This is a false economy. If the bike doesn't fit, you will never be able to ride to the best of your abilities. And everything matters: the saddle position (fore and aft); the height you sit over the pedal; the handlebar reach and drop. The elements that comprise a good fit are numerous and they must come together to create an exact fit – they cannot be approximated. Textbooks and drawing boards can tell you some of the story, but experience is definitely the key to sizing and fitting a cyclist to a frame, as Italian frame builder Dario Pegoretti explains:

'Everybody wants a chart of my geometry. In reality, when I say 73°, it is not really, so it is really stupid that I write on the chart… 72.55° – it has no sense. I was very lucky because in my work a big experience was with a young team called Riboli who were based in Ilasi. I was working very, very closely with them. From 1980 to 1985 it was one of the most important young teams in Italy. Davide Rebellin rode for the team when he was young. This was a good experience because I was free. It was a different experience – different from a pro team who always supply you with

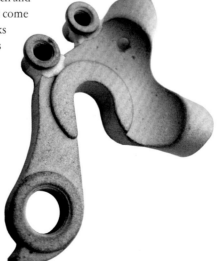

a list and you just build the frames. Sometimes there is a top pro rider who comes to the shop and asks for an opinion, but normally not, it's not a stupid job... but it's not very exciting. But this job, with 20 riders, I started in January and every year or two it changed. I remember in two months I'd build 20 frames. It is very exciting – the guys take the bike and ride the bike. I remember I'd take the scooter to ride with them as they trained – to have an opinion on their fit. This was very important and I think this was a great experience.'

Find a fit expert you feel comfortable with. A good bike-fit technician will take several hours on your fit, and some, like Dario Pegoretti, might even jump on a scooter and ride alongside you to make sure you're pedalling efficiently on the frame he has built. It's unlikely that a builder will go to these lengths now, but whatever route you have decided to take, you must listen to the fitter's advice. Fitters will recognize what will work within certain parameters and what alterations can be made without sacrificing handling or comfort. Consider, first and foremost, what type of riding you are going to do before making a purchase. Make sure that the bike is perfect for you, never try to make any old bike do things that it wasn't designed to do as the results will be disappointing. The most popular bikes bought are often those ridden by the professional teams and this means that riders will make decisions based on what is fashionable rather than what is suitable. A professional rider's requirements for a bicycle are very different from yours. Spending your working life on a bicycle would mean that (apart from getting very fit) you would be able to cope with a more race-orientated position, and if you are new to cycling or untrained, this position can be very uncomfortable and highly inappropriate.

Eddy Merckx was pedantic about his saddle height, even adjusting it mid-race if he wasn't happy. One thing that most professional riders have in common is an almost pathological obsession with their position, and a tape measure and a small notebook with their sizes and specification always travels with them. Their mechanics will have all these details too. You should take as much care with getting this right as they do. Expensive components are useless if set up wrongly. Once you have the size dialled into your bike, make sure you copy this across to all your other bikes. Use the same saddle, pedals, handlebar type and even brand of control lever, wherever possible. There is no point riding in a position all winter just to change it completely when you wheel your race bike out of the shed in the spring.

INJURY ISSUES

Previous injury will definitely influence how you sit and pedal on the bike. Injuries can't be resolved with a custom-built bike but they can be accommodated and considered during the fit process. A bad back, a stiff neck, a sore shoulder or a dodgy knee may all be symptoms of a poor fit, but they are more likely to be pointers to a weakness or previous injury that needs treatment, some remedial stretching and, perhaps, even physiotherapy. Experts in the biomechanics of cycling will be able to help, and the frame builder will certainly be able to consider these issues and advise how to set you up to minimize the problem. Finding out why these things hurt is all part of making your cycling more enjoyable and, it is hoped, faster. A properly fitted and well-made bicycle will offer many years' good service. This may mean that as you get stronger and the nature of your riding changes, your fit will need to be reassessed. Having a close relationship with your builder and fit technician is essential, as it will help you to make informed and accurate tweaks to your set-up.

Frame Geometry

Frame angles vary from bike to bike and frame builders have dramatically different ideas about what works best. The double diamond shape has remained the same for over a century and this long history of design has allowed builders to learn that subtle tweaks in angles can make a huge difference. Styles in frame angles have changed – the slacker seat and head angles were once used to combat poor road surfaces and, although they are still used on touring or cyclo-cross bikes, which need to be more comfortable, as roads have improved so, too, the geometry of the road bike has developed to allow the best blend of responsive handling and rider comfort.

Seat tube length

Seat tubes are the size that defines the overall quoted size of a bike. There are many ways to measure the frame and each manufacturer may have a different technique. 'Stock' off-the-peg frames are never the same standard measurement. This isn't a huge problem for a good bike fitter as the seat tube has the benefit of an adjustable seat post that can be adjusted to cope with leg length (see seat tube angles, opposite). However, it can mean that you 'fall between' sizes and a stock bike just won't fit. For example, you may want a 55cm (21⅜in) seat tube with a 56cm (22in) top tube, but the nearest sized mass-produced monocoque frame will be a 53cm (20⅘in) seat tube with a 55cm (21⅜in) top tube. The next size up is a 56cm (22in) seat tube with a 57cm (22⅖in) top tube. To get the right length you have to compromise the seat tube length, which also dictates the height of the head tube. So the result is a compromise. Don't compromise.

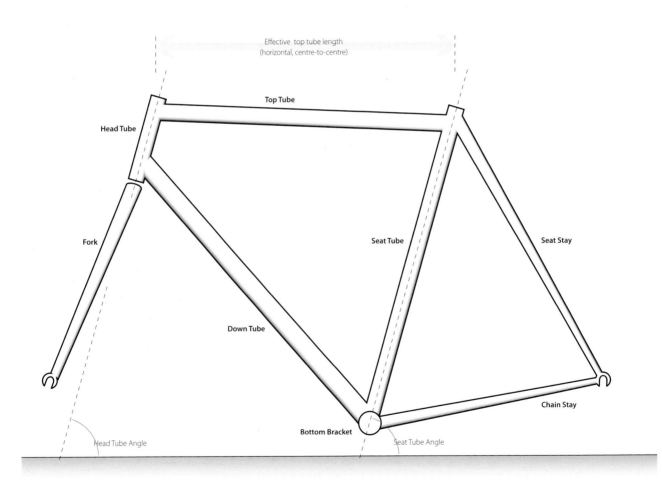

Top tube length

In my opinion this is the key measurement of a road bike and will be the hardest measurement to alter or accommodate after the frame has been built. A 'square' frame (with a seat tube length matching the length of the top tube) is a good starting point, but arm length, torso length and even leg length all influence the length of the top tube. For example, a bike with a 54cm (21⅛in) seat tube could have a top tube length of anything from 53 to 58cm (20⅘ to 22⅘ins), which is a fairly broad range. Stem length can alter the reach of the bike but over-long frames can be slightly pedestrian in their handling and really short top tubes can create problems with twitchy steering. A shorter front end can also create problems with pedal overlap. To make matters even more complicated all frame builders take a different approach to measuring the top tube, and it is harder to define in compact frames and those that have unusual top tube designs.

Head tube angles

The head angle governs the feel of the steering and is also directly influenced by the size and rake of the fork and the length of the stem. The standard modern road-race bike will usually go for a head angle of around 73°. Slacker head angles below 73° are used on touring bikes and can be used on cyclo-cross bikes, where all-day comfort and rough riding will benefit from slowing the steering slightly.

Seat tube angles

To match the seat angle to the rider a builder will need to consider many issues to get it exactly right. Your leg length and foot position over the pedals influences the angle, but as the seat post adjusts for height, it can also adjust for a wide range of saddle positions (fore and aft). A neutral road-riding position will usually be achieved with a 73° seat angle, although a slacker seat angle can be used to accommodate a more laid back position.

BEYOND GEOMETRY

The one thing that isn't usually apparent when you first look at a bike is what frame angles the builder has incorporated into the head and seat angles. You will usually have to ask and the answer you get may not be precise. It will depend on the materials too, as Dario Pegoretti explains again:

'Many people in the world think there is the absolute geometry. It doesn't exist, because if there is an absolute geometry everybody must be on the same frame and this is not possible. I think when you decide to build a frame you must consider geometry, material, diameter of the tubes, the use and what you want from the frame. But geometry alone is just one part of the frame. If you take two tubesets, cut the tubes and place them in the same jig, probably you have two frames completely the same. But if you change the tubes in one, the diameters, the two frames ride completely differently, so it is not just a question of geometry. If you change just one important tube like the down tube, you have a different frame with the same geometry. If you use very thin tubesets they can absorb and flex more than a fatter tube. Then they would change because, during a ride, the frame moves. If it is a rigid structure, it cannot move – movement of the frame is dependent on diameter and on the material. And if you try to use a thin tube the angle between the head and the down tube changes when you take a bump in the road – it can move more than a beefy one… and you can have the 'same' comfort with a stiff material and a slacker angle, perhaps.'

Compact frame shape

Compact or sloping geometry is based on that of the mountain bike frame design. Championed by Mike Burrows (a bicycle designer with Giant in the early 1990s, who had developed much of the technology behind Chris Boardman's Lotus-built pursuit bike), the compact frame had been developed earlier as an idea by many independent frame builders. Mountain bikes need a higher front end than road bikes as they need a more upright position for negotiating off-road trails. They also need clearance from the top tube, so it has to slope from the higher head tube to the shorter seat tube. The premise with compact geometry wasn't just about individual fit, but more about having fewer frame sizes and being able to tune to the fit using longer seat posts and adjustable stems. For those riders in the middle of the size option this was fine, but the bike became compromised when used by very small or very tall riders. As a rule, big frames will flex more than small frames, so many taller riders like to use a compact frame to increase the rigidity. This can also facilitate a higher front end when combined with a longer head tube.

Standard frame shape

Although sloping designs are the current fashion, flat top tubes are the traditional shape for road bikes and are making a comeback in frame designs. Many riders feel that they are more stable than compact frames and offer a less 'direct' ride, handle better on rougher roads and require a little less rider input to steer them. I ride both and I prefer standard geometry for long days on the bike, however compact.

STIFFNESS

Stiffness is a much maligned term when defining a bicycle. Performance bicycles are built with many types of frame tubing and geometry that can be adjusted to provide the rider with the required level of power transfer and comfort. Combining the two has been a challenge for builders and getting one right means that the other will inevitably suffer. As with all frame issues a builder will be able to apply techniques and materials to match your requirements.

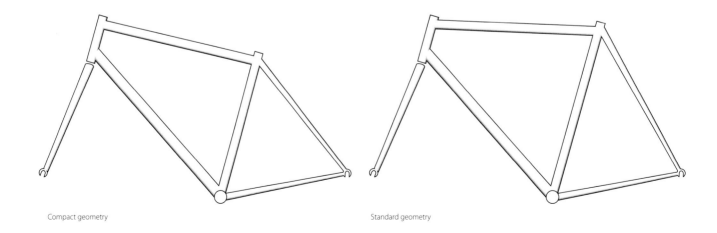

Compact geometry

Standard geometry

Geometry anomalies

Road frames look for a neutral geometry, one that can cope with a number of racing and riding situations and demands. Track, time trial, touring and cyclo-cross frames all differ slightly in the hardware that the frame needs to accommodate the riding characteristics of these disciplines.

TIME TRIAL

Time trial specialists now use a handlebar with extensions that allow the rider to rest in an aero tuck. The rider's position will differ considerably from the standard road riding position, so the geometry is very different. Road bikes can be converted into time trial bikes (sometimes using small compact frames instead of standard sized versions) but this is often a compromise as the lower bar height needed is difficult to achieve on a standard frame. Custom time trial frames usually have a steeper seat angle that places the rider further forward on the bike to maximize power output (see also page 16).

TRACK

Because track events are usually shorter than road races, most of the focus for a track racer is transfer of power and aerodynamics. However, keen track riders also ride the road, so many copy their road position almost exactly. Control of the bike is also important, so don't be tempted just to fit the deepest set of drops you can find just because this is what the professional sprinters do. Look for a balanced position first and think about aerodynamics later. Lower, more powerful saddle heights are popular because the hands are usually placed on the drops. The frame geometry is sharper and more aggressive than a road bike, so the track frame seat and head angle are steeper, the chainstays are shorter and the forks are less raked, giving a much tighter, more responsive machine (see also page 20).

CYCLO-CROSS

The obvious difference with a cyclo-cross frame's geometry is a slightly taller bike than one that is used on the road. Generally speaking the geometry is slacker than a road bike with a longer wheelbase, shorter top tube and higher bottom bracket (see also page 24).

Materials

Materials also play a large part in how a frame is built, which is why custom-built frames are made from materials that are easy to work. Builders have preferred materials, often dictated by their experience and skill. Materials cost does influence the result too, so a really good, well-fitted steel frame may cost the same as a poorly-made off-the-peg carbon frame. The important thing is that the bike's quality is defined by the way it is made rather than by the material it is made from. All frames have certain characteristics that are due to the materials from which they are made.

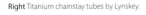

Right Titanium chainstay tubes by Lynskey.

Steel

Steel is the traditional material for making bicycle frames. Unfortunately, at entry level there are only a few available – because, try as hard as they might, the manufacturers can't make an aluminium frame with the same strength, longevity and ride characteristics. If you can, always buy a steel bike first – it will last several years and can be used as a winter trainer if you intend to buy a more expensive second bike later on. Custom-frame builders usually work in steel, because it is arguably the most adaptable material. Reynolds, Dedacciai, Columbus and True Temper all make excellent steel tubing for bicycles – Dedacciai Zero One is just as light as comparable aluminium tubes. Construction of steel frames is usually with double-butted tubes (internally shaped, with thinner sections in the middle to save weight and thicker sections at the ends to increase strength). These are brazed and lugged at the joints; some builders use silver solder for some applications. TIG (tungsten inert gas) welded steel frames are usually made from lightweight triple butted tubes and these days 8.1-kg (18-lb) steel bikes are possible. Stainless steel has become more readily available and Reynolds' 953 tubeset has created the potential for a steel frame to match the strength of titanium with similar corrosion resistance and longevity.

Good:
Steel is easy to custom build and it's simple to repair tubes.

Bad:
Corrosion can affect steel and it's the heaviest material for frames.

Aluminium

Aluminium is the cheapest bike-building material, which is why the market is flooded with hundreds of different types and models. On the plus side this means they are very competitively priced and you can get a lot for a little money, but on the minus side they can be uncomfortably 'stiff' and are generally supplied by mainstream manufacturers in fewer sizes (usually S, M & L). So always remember to check the geometry before you buy as some frames are made to very strange specifications. The numbers quoted next to the material description denotes their alloy, with the T suffix relating to the heat treatment, for example 7075-T6. As with steel, butted aluminium is stronger and lighter and quality frames are heat treated after welding to ensure maximum strength. Many cheap aluminium frames are not. Find out how a frame has been made before you buy. Tubing from Dedacciai, Easton and Columbus tubes are at the quality end of the aluminium market.

Good:
Aluminium is cheap, light and strong.

Bad:
It can provide a harsh ride and longevity can be questionable (although this is not an issue with quality higher-end tubesets). Lighter tubes are easily damaged and are often difficult and expensive to repair.

Titanium

The wonder material for bike building – or so you might think – titanium is as light as aluminium, as strong as steel and as comfortable too. But you have to be a very good frame builder to build a good titanium bike – it's a very difficult material to work with. So be very wary of cheap titanium frames as cheap titanium is not as perfect as you might think and there have been some questionable bikes built in the past. Titanium is a high-end material, with unparalleled corrosion resistance. It should not be considered a budget bike option, as you will have to compromise too much on the components. Titanium for bike tubing comes in two main types: 3AL-2.5V and 6AL-4V. 3AL-2.5V is an alloy consisting of 3% aluminium, 2.5% vanadium, and 94.5% pure titanium. It's also known as grade 9. It's easily formable, has excellent corrosion resistance and superb fatigue life. This makes 3AL-2.5V the type most used when making a bike frame. 6AL-4V is better quality, but more difficult to work.

Good:
Titanium is very light and strong and, best of all, longevity is not an issue.

Bad:
It's an expensive option and is difficult to repair.

Carbon Fibre

Carbon fibre frames are made either in a mould or from tubes held together with lugs and glue. Carbon is the only material that has no recognized frame builders' standard, although some tubing manufacturers now have tubesets made that can be supplied as kits for builders to assemble. Carbon fibre is less flexible than metal in construction techniques and specialist equipment is needed to realize successful designs. Be wary of cheap carbon frames, which usually use moulding processes or tubes made from poorly prepared material, often with more resin than carbon in the build process.

Good:
Carbon fibre frames are very, very light, very responsive and comfortable.

Bad:
It's expensive and difficult to repair, and it cannot be recycled.

Right Carbon fibre can be formed and glued into virtually any shape.

Dropouts, Frame Components and Lugs

The double diamond pattern frame is widely regarded as the perfect design for bicycles and it is the shape that is accepted by bike racers and organizations as the recognized configuration. So, whatever material you use, the components that make up the frame are the same; they may be joined differently but, generally speaking, hand-built frames use tubes, cut to length and either joined by lugs or perfectly mitred and welded at the joins.

DROPOUTS AND FORK ENDS

There is a distinct difference between the two basic designs in dropout. Horizontal dropouts are usually used on traditional frames that will often be built with long horizontal slots in their dropouts. These were used for several practical reasons – to align the wheel perfectly and to allow for wider section tyres and some wheel adjustment front to rear. Vertical dropouts are now more regularly used on road bikes. They're designed to make wheel installation easier and also to prevent the wheel being 'pulled' when pedalling. Track bikes use rear-facing fork ends with 120mm (4⅜in) spacing. These are used because they allow for easy adjustment of chain tension and also so that the wheel can be easily removed when the frame clearances are very tight. They differ from standard road-bike dropouts in that they have longer slots to cope with changing different gear ratios and the angle at which they are positioned is perfectly parallel with the ground, so that the geometry stays constant when moving the wheel backwards and forwards in the fork ends.

SEAT LUGS

The seat lug is also a very important join in the frame and an area that can be problematic. Aluminium and titanium seat stays are usually secured 'fastback', that is without any seat lug at all, and the seat post is then secured with a separate collar. Some steel frames use this technique, which saves a little weight but isn't as neat as an integrated seat cluster lug.

HEAD LUGS

The point at which the frame tubes meet the head tube is perhaps the most important join on the bike. The head lugs are usually made from pressed or cast steel and the specific head-tube angle is usually predetermined by their shape. Investment cast lugs, most notably by Henry James, are now most popular. Hand-cut lugs and fancy styles are available, if that's your thing.

BOTTOM BRACKET SHELL

This is the engine room of the bike. The standard has been set for many decades and threading will depend on the origin of the bracket shell. Italian and English threads are the most popular and differ slightly in thread pitch. The big difference is that the Italian bottom bracket has two right-hand threads, while the English has a left-hand thread on the drive (crank) side of the bracket shell. Neither is better, in my experience, although if the threads are poorly prepared or the bracket is insufficiently tight in the frame, Italian brackets can unwind when pedalling. Always check the size of the threads before attempting to remove them or specifying a new unit. Steel bikes can have a variety of types of bottom bracket shells. Cinelli and Everest make very nice ones.

Opposite: from top, left to right Cast fork crown, head tube lug, Campagnolo horizontal touring dropouts, cast bottom bracket shell, Campagnolo fork end, Campagnolo short horizontal dropout.

Head tube

The head tube holds the fork and headset in place. The height of the head tube varies from frame to frame and this needs to be considered in the bike-fit process. Extended head tubes can be added to prevent the use of lots of Aheadset spacers, improving headset function and longevity.

Down tube

The down tube braces the head tube to the bottom bracket. Tubes with a fatter diameter are popular as this can add considerable stability to the bottom bracket. Many builders build in extra stiffness here by swaging the tube at either end to facilitate its welding to the head tube and bottom bracket.

Seat stays

The seat stays brace the rear wheel to the top of the seat tube. How they join the seat tube is the subject of much debate. Stays on steel bikes can be spear-shaped, wraparound, shot-in (flush to the seat tube) or mono-stay. Seat stays need to be carefully chosen if you want the frame to be comfortable, especially if the chainstays are beefy. Seat stays may be reinforced or shaped on cyclo-cross and touring frames that use cantilever brakes, to accommodate the geometry of the brake and to brace the seat stays against the increased braking forces.

Chainstays

The length of the chainstays can make a tremendous difference to how the bike handles – longer chainstays add extra comfort, shorter stays make for quicker handling and pedalling reaction. The shape of the stays at the bottom bracket is significant – fatter stays can add extra stability, especially for out-of-the-saddle riding.

Top tube

Compact or sloping geometry will see the top tube slope slightly. It will usually be built lugless, because modifying lugs to deal with the change of angles at the head lug and seat lug creates difficulties. As a very general rule traditional geometry with a flat top tube is still the preferred method for many steel frame builders, and sloping geometry is more popular in the modern TIG welded materials such as stainless steel, aluminium and titanium.

Seat tube

The seat tube determines the size of the frame and although this is adjustable with the seat post it still has to be critically measured to allow for perfect frame fit. The seat tube is the anchor point for the other main tubes and stays. Structurally it has less significance (some frames interrupt this tube and experimental carbon fibre frames have removed it completely) but in handmade frames it still has a significant role.

BOTTLE CAGE BOSSES

Twin bottle cage bosses are usually added to most road frames. Track and cyclo-cross racing frames usually don't have any, although cyclo-cross bikes can have them added if you want to use the frame for longer rides.

FRONT DERAILLEUR BRAZE-ON

Steel frames can have a small bracket brazed on to the seat tube to attach the front derailleur to. This is a neat touch and prevents the damage the clamp on a standard derailleur can cause to the paintwork. However, it can create problems when fitting peculiar gear ratios so consider this when the frame is made.

The Frame

Construction Processes

Steel
The oldest method of bike building is complicated yet perfectly resolved. Steel frames are usually joined together with lugs, which can be joined with either bronze brazing rod or silver solder. Popular tubesets with lugged frames that were used traditionally included Reynolds (531 and 853) and Columbus SL and SLX. TIG welding became popular in the 1990s and lighter frames were possible from more technically advanced steel tubes. Contemporary versions of these are Dedacciai's Zero Replica and Columbus' Spirit tubesets. Stainless steel is now becoming popular – although expensive it has all the qualities of steel and the longevity of titanium. Reynolds 953 and Columbus XCr are the most popular.

As riders attempted to get lighter frames, frame builders dropped the lugs altogether. The lugless brazing technique needs careful cutting or mitreing of the tubes so that they are perfectly joined at the tube. Whether this saves any weight over a good pair of lightweight lugs is questionable and the choice is down to personal preference.

Many steel manufacturers now use TIG welding to join tubes. It's fast and strong and can be applied to several types of material, including steel, aluminium and titanium. Some traditional steel builders will not build a frame this way, preferring to braze, but exponents of TIG welding can make lighter frames from larger section tubes that can be joined in a much freer way. In this way frames can be realized with various tube diameters to cope with the different stresses in the frame.

Titanium
Titanium is extremely difficult to weld and almost impossible to braze, so the recognized and most used technique for making titanium frames is TIG welding. This allows for a very lightweight frame with very little extra material needed to join the frame tubes. However, it's difficult to hide your mistakes on unfinished materials like titanium, so welders need a lot of experience and a familiarity with the material. As a result, good titanium frames are usually made by very good welders.

Top An inside view of lugless steel brazing.
Right Fancy lugs allow for ornate steel construction.

Aluminium

Aluminium frames were first joined together with lugs and glue although the resulting frames were flexible and unreliable. Until the late 1980s welding was strictly reserved for the most expensive aluminium frames, then TIG welding technology took a leap forward and the equipment became cheaper. The huge boom in mountain bikes meant that the big Far-Eastern builders started welding aluminium bikes for large bike producers. Aluminium is cheap and easy to weld, and although it is difficult to weld it well, the Taiwanese perfected it and started making much cheaper frames readily available. Good aluminium frames are hard to find and the material needs careful selection – look out for Scandium tubes by Easton and Dedacciai's SC 6110 A-T6 and 7003-T6 tubesets.

Carbon fibre

Carbon fibre cannot be welded, so it has to be glued together. The best way to make custom-fitted carbon frames is with separate tubes and lugs, just like a steel frame. The big difference is that all carbon frames have to be glued and heat treated (to harden the glue). Most manufacturers have their own heat-curing methods and many are closely guarded secrets. This technique was pioneered by Ernesto Colnago in 1994 on his groundbreaking C40 frame, the first carbon frame that could be easily custom-built to the individual rider's specification. This is the process that all the carbon builders use today.

Top Aluminium welds on display.
Left A lugged carbon frame.

Richard Sachs Cycles

No. 73, Hastings Pond Road
Warwick
MA 01378
USA
www.richardsachs.com
+1 978 544 1842

When you first see a Richard Sachs bike you are drawn closer into it immediately. The perfect lugwork, the square shoulders to the fork crowns, the matter-of-fact simple lines and the thick paint all contribute to its simple beauty. I've drooled over many bikes, but there is something unique about a Richard Sachs bike.

Some may want frames to look retro, but there is something different about a Sachs frame and something distinctly modern about them too. The closest you get to them is from the traditional steel builders in Japan. One of these, Yoshiaki Nagasawa, is renowned as a frame building heavyweight, a genius in the art of hand brazing and clearly an influence on Sachs (who also happens to own several Nagasawa frames). Sachs first spotted Nagasawa at a New York bike show and he had to track him down. Why? 'I was inspired by the Japanese reverence for quality handmade articles of any and all types, some important, some mundane, but all constructed with respect for craft, skill and heritage, and, I suspect, with little or no regard paid to commerce or promotion. My attitude towards frame building embraces this attitude.'

Richard Sachs has been building bicycle frames since 1972. He still works alone, hence the very long wait for one of his frames. He selects the geometry, cuts and brazes the tubes, files the lugs, he does everything necessary to complete the eight to ten frames he builds each month. Ride-wise Richard Sachs has a wealth of knowledge from racing himself, so, yes, they ride well, as he affirms, in his own modest words.

'What I do build are rationally designed, precisely constructed, hand-finished road racing frames. I use a proprietary blend of Columbus PegoRichie tubing along with the finest investment cast, forged and pressed steel fittings available. Through the years I have been able to combine my experience in the sport with my artisan approach to frame building to develop a predictable, repeatable construction assembly that enables me to produce a perfectly straight, well-balanced frame.'

'Some may want frames to look retro, but there is something different about a Sachs frame and something distinctly modern about them too.'

Materials used:

PegoRichie tubing – a collaboration between Dario Pegoretti and myself to design a twenty-first-century iteration of a material that can be joined with lugs and have all the weight, strength and emotional characteristics that are expected in bicycles made in the ateliers of frame builders who still do their own work rather than source it from Asia.

Employees:

One – Richard Sachs.

Price range:

Frames from US$4,000 and complete bicycles from US$8,000 (as of December 2008).

Waiting period (average!):

Currently, delivery is quoted at seven years.

Frames built per year:

50–60 per year, not counting RS Cyclo-cross Team frames.

Who are your customers and how would you 'define' them?

My customer is an amalgam of someone who is discerning, not swayed by marketing, has a sense of the industry's history, doesn't want to be made a monkey of, 'gets it', is in no rush, and more. Many of my clients call in many times before committing. From where I sit, they research this well and know intimately what they want and need and have no issues queuing up for it.

How long have you been building bikes?

I went to London in 1972, and in late 1975 I started Richard Sachs Cycles.

Do you make (or have you made) frames for any professional riders or teams?

Yes (on the latter). But these are different times. Prior to the last decade or so, I could count as many as 30 riders on RS bicycles who were on the national, world, and Olympic teams of the USA and Canada. For me, or more aptly stated, for 'us', all of that ended when the federations began to mandate that riders had to use parts and brands from the official equipment pool from whoever threw money at it in any particular year.

What started your interest in bicycle engineering/design?

That is too long a story. Suffice to say it was not/never planned. It was all serendipitous. I ended up in London after being turned down for a measly wrench job for which I was never qualified anyway! Learning about bicycles and moving overseas was an act of revenge (to that shop) as much as anything else.

Who taught you to build?

For the most part, I am self-taught. A year in London at Witcomb Lightweight Cycles set the table for me, but I was not there as an apprentice. I witnessed and absorbed as much as one could, but once I came to Connecticut and jump-started my career, nothing I did had much overlap with what I saw there.

Who influences what you do now (if not all of the above)?

I have influences in this industry. I did long ago. Bill Hurlow was one. The legend surrounding Faliero and Alberto Masi and their artisan shop at the Vigorelli was another. Mr Nagasawa also is in the mix. But all of that is mostly

residual stuff from the 1970s and early 1980s. Since then I have taken whatever cues I took from outside industry sources. Most of all, it's fantasy coupled with mild low self-esteem. I have always wondered what existed in places I had no access to, and the antidote was to create a mythical worker who could channel experiences and design elements so that I could, somehow, eventually morph into that. Suffice to say, working alone is its own reward, yet can come with a few demons too!

What is the best material for frame manufacturing (and why)?
Steel. Because I am comfortable with it and can tame it – period.

How do you size your customers?
Intuitively.

What is the most exciting new development in frame design or tubing technology?
The PegoRichie tubeset, now in its third iteration and available in two weights and two lengths, tops that list.

What's the most important element to the frame?
Design trumps all. Construction and material compete for second and third place! I don't build concept bikes, trade show samples or unrideable prototypes. I don't choose the latest angles for this season's riding position. And I don't change my material choice, tube shape, or joining process with each new model year.

What do you want to achieve for your customers?
I have never considered that. I continue to make these frames to better understand why so many become what they want, rather than what is planned. To be sure, all frames fit, work well and please the client, but making something by hand, particularly an item wound so tight as is a steel bicycle frame, includes a certain amount of acquiescing to the material and the process. After 30 years, it still confounds me that no two can be alike, and my role at the workbench is to take the better of the two and repeat it. And so it goes...

Who is/was the best frame manufacturer or builder and why?
Frames are things, and there's no real way to account for them unless a rider is part of the equation. To wit, there is not and will never be a 'best'.

Steering

Forks

As the roads have improved so too have bicycle forks. In the early days of the Tour de France forks were huge, brittle and unreliable, roads were rough and tarmac was rare. Rough roads meant that riders used long-wheelbased bikes with fat tyres, so that while bikes may have been more comfortable than they are now, they were, like early mountain bikes, heavy and sluggish to handle.

Fork design had a big influence on this handling and, although the materials available were basic, the geometry was tweaked to gain the best mix of comfort and handling that would, in turn, result in faster speeds. The problem with the bikes prior to the 1960s was that they didn't turn corners as a result of long wheelbases and long forks.

However, as steel tubing became more reliable, forks could be made lighter and more responsive, and as roads got better the rake of the fork was reduced and the comfort afforded with longer 'springier' fork blades was less of a prerequisite. Experiments with geometry through the 1970s and 1980s has resulted in a standard fork for road racing (depending on frame size) and, combined with a recognized frame geometry and standardized wheel size, fork design is now as much about the materials as it is about the dimensions.

Left Carbon fibre road fork .
Opposite Straight-bladed steel.

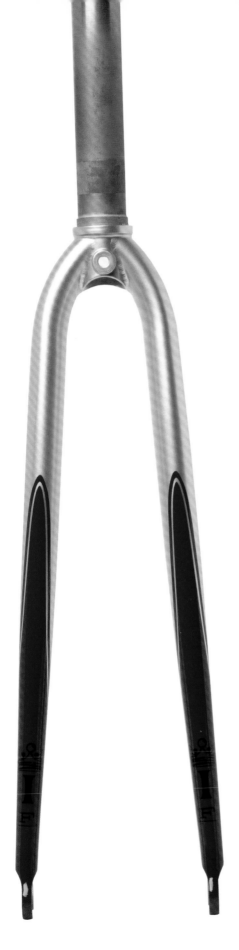

Steel forks

Steel forks are a reliable option. Although heavier than carbon fibre forks they have beneficial properties for a smoother ride and, arguably, for more predictable handling over rough roads. Many top frame builders, such as Richard Sachs, use a steel fork to complement the geometry of the bike and to do this successfully needs a high level of understanding and skill. Readymade steel and carbon replacement forks may seem to be an easier option (which is probably why many frame builders use them) but they will not match all frames in the same way that a hand-built pair will. Some carbon forks are therefore built specifically to frame manufacturers' exact requirements and it is always essential to replace these with the correct specification fork.

Straight-bladed forks

These forks, known as 'power forks', were popularized by Ernesto Colnago and other Italian builders in the early 1990s. They used a straight blade and angled the rake by offsetting the fork angle at the fork crown. The result was supposedly a more direct handling fork that didn't suffer (as was popularly believed) from a harsher ride by using tapered and sometimes triple-butted steel tubes. Although the idea was perhaps a triumph of style over substance, they could be made slightly lighter than curved-rake forks and, more importantly, were easier to build. However, this move away from traditionally curved fork blades did change the development of the fork, and as fork makers (notably Dario Pegoretti) started to experiment with better tubing and TIG welding they ditched the crown lug and started joining the two fork blades together in what became known as the uni-crown design, which saved a lot of weight and made the fork noticeably stiffer.

Carbon forks

Replacing steel fork blades with carbon fibre took some doing when they first started to appear in the mid-1990s, especially as 'consumer' manufacturing with carbon composites was still in its infancy. Forks were primitive and needed aluminium parts for the steerer and the fork crown, with the carbon blades bonded into place. Moulds and bonding processes were a closely guarded secret, but as manufacturing caught up specialist fork makers came up with huge weight savings over the standard steel fork. Carbon forks can add a certain amount of rigidity to the steering especially when sprinting, but they can also have harsh riding characteristics and, when combined with oversized bars and stems, can provide painful results on long rides and over cobblestones. Aluminium fork crowns and steerers are now used only in cheaper carbon forks, as full carbon forks are now made in moulds and with more reliable materials.

Cyclo-cross

Cyclo-cross fork demands are different from those of roadgoing forks. The general principle is to allow for a longer wheelbase in a cyclo-cross bike. The fork is also designed for more mud clearance around the fork crown, so it is usually longer than a fork made for road racing. But, more importantly, a gentle, longer rake (up to 55mm/2¼ins) provides a smoother ride over rough roads and terrain. As cyclo-cross races have become faster and, arguably, less technical so bikes have become more like road bikes in their geometry. Cyclo-cross brakes mean that integrating bosses for cantilever brakes has taken a while for the carbon manufacturers to get right, but carbon cyclo-cross forks now offer a very light alternative to steel.

Left Steel cyclo-cross fork.
Opposite Carbon fibre cyclo-cross fork.

Rake and Trail

While these two related terms are often confused they refer to slightly different aspects of the frame's geometry. Both have a direct effect on the handling characteristics of the bike, but they are determined by the angle of the frame's head tube, which usually depends on the overall size of the frame and purpose for which it has been built.

In simple terms, the rake defines the curve of the fork. The size specified is basically the distance between the position where the fork ends (where the hub is secured into the bike) away from the centre line of the steering column (usually referred to as the steerer). Although some frame builders refer to this as an angle rather than a measurement, in modern racing bikes fork manufacturers refer to it as a measurement and this is usually somewhere between 40 and 50mm (1½ and 2ins). Which size your bike uses will be determined by the frame's geometry.

The trail is a slightly more academic concept and is determined by the distance from the centre line of the steerer where it would reach the ground away from the point of contact of the tyre with the ground. Trail can make a huge difference to the handling of a bike. It is directly influenced by the fork rake and the angle of the head tube. Less trail (with a slacker head angle) slows the steering and more trail (with a steeper head angle) provides a quicker handling frame. There are many influences on this and, as a result, working out the exact geometry of it is impossible (for example tyre size, profile and pressure can have a dramatic effect, as can braking and turning forces). For this reason fork rake is an easier and more accessible way to determine fork geometry.

The frame head angles and the overall size of the bike will determine what fork rake your bike uses. A very big frame needs less rake to keep the steering neutral and a very small frame may need a longer rake. Some builders (including Colnago) use the same fork throughout their range – 51–65cm (2–2½in) standard sizes, in Colnago's case – and alter the head tube geometry to suit, which is why it's always important to seek out manufacturers' guidance and frame geometries when changing forks.

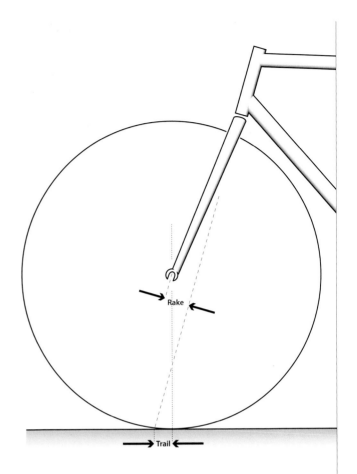

Pedal overlap

As frames became shorter and geometry steeper, the front wheel moved closer to the point where the feet rotated. This is not much of a problem if the bike is used at faster speeds (where steering is more subtle and the wheel moves less to change direction) but at slower speeds and for tight turning the foot could hit the front wheel and create problems. Fixed wheel road going bikes need to take account of this aspect, especially for city riding where there may be a lot of slow speed turning. It's worth noting that track racing frames have very close clearances, and because steering is at a minimum pedal overlap is not really an issue, which is another reason why track frames make for bad road bikes.

FORK INSTALLATION

All manufacturers will issue instructions but generally speaking all forks follow a similar installation process:

- Aheadsets need to be installed with the right tools and preferably by an experienced mechanic who will face and prepare the frame appropriately.

- Crown-bearing installation on carbon forks is of paramount importance and the correct tools must be used. Bodged installation of this part can result in fork failure.

- Once the steerer has been cut to size and the fork has been installed it cannot be lengthened, so cutting it in a hurry can prove expensive.

- Spacer stacks under the Aheadstem should be limited to 30mm (1¼ins). Anything bigger probably means that the frame's head tube needs to be taller to accommodate your position.

- Always use the correct bung to secure the Aheadset top cap. Never use a bung from a different fork (especially those used with steel steerers).

Fork failure

There are many theories as to why forks fail. In my experience the main weakening factor is installation and damage caused when assembling the headset parts, so for this reason always have the forks assembled by an experienced technician. Once the assembly is together try to leave the Aheadstem in place, as removing it (if, for example, you have to pack the bike for travel) can scratch the steerer. Carbon fibres are particularly sensitive to scratches and the compression damage usually associated with overtightening of the Aheadstem. This damage creates scoring of the material and this in turn makes for stress risers that can result in cracks or delamination of the material and, at worst, failure of the steerer. Crashes that impact the handlebars can also result in damage to the steerer column, so always have this checked out when you stack the bike. Remember when George Hincapie's carbon forks snapped in the 2006 Paris–Roubaix? It was believed that the headset parts came loose in an earlier crash and the resulting damage to the steerer meant that the fork column failed catastrophically – it was not the fault of the parts or the mechanics, just down to the nature of the race and the fact that all parts need to be checked properly after crashing. Never ride Paris–Roubaix with a loose headset.

Steel forks can fail too, usually when they are neglected. The head tube can seal in water and the result will be a rusty steerer, which is how the integrity of the fork begins to deteriorate. Keep a close eye on steel forks for any signs of rust and replace them. Head-on impacts will often mean that the forks should be replaced. In such circumstances, steel forks will probably bend, so the damage is often visible; whereas carbon forks can appear intact, but the steerer may absorb the impact and be weakened by hard impacts. Again, check it all thoroughly and have the parts stripped and rebuilt regularly by an experienced mechanic. If in doubt have a new pair fitted as failure in the forks can result in serious injuries. Many fork and bike manufacturers will offer a crash replacement policy, so check before you buy a replacement pair as such a 'warranty' can reduce the cost.

Headsets and Aheadsets

The mountain bike can stake a claim in the invention of the Aheadset in the late 1980s, with Dia Compe holding the current patent, but I have seen pictures of such an arrangement that go back over half a century. As with most bicycle 'inventions' nothing is as new as it first appears.

Traditionally road bike fork steerers were 2.5cm (1in) in diameter, so before Aheadset forks, the fork steerers on road bikes were threaded and fastened into the frame with a headset. The handlebar stem was retained into the steerer tube with a quill or wedge stem system, which was crude but effective. Standard quill-fitting stems and headsets are now rare – they worked well but required specialist headset spanners to adjust. The quill stem is less serviceable than an Aheadset as it's harder to remove the bars without taking off all the bar tape and the brake levers. However, a quill stem offers larger ranges of adjustment than the Aheadset system and looks oh-so-right on a retro-look bike.

The 2.5cm (1in), threaded-type headset is rarely used these days and most road bikes now have a slightly larger 2.8cm (1⅛in) Aheadset, which has since become the industry standard. The Aheadset is a very simple component and the unit is therefore relatively easy to maintain and service, usually with allen keys rather than the large headset spanners that were used during the years when the industry used the threaded headset. The Aheadset system consists of two bearing races positioned at either end of the head tube. The races run in these bearings and are held in place by the fork crown at one end and the stem at the other. Adjustment is made with a compression top cap that is secured into the steerer – the handlebar stem clamps the system together and prevents it all coming loose.

The latest integrated head tube frame design, where the head tube is flared top and bottom to accept the bearing parts into the frame, has meant that the head tubes can be made larger in diameter. I never thought that these would catch

Lock nut – this threads onto the steering column and holds the bearing parts in adjustment.

Washer – usually has a tooth that locates into a slot on the threaded steerer column, it allows the lock nut to rotate independently when tightening onto the top bearing cup.

Top bearing cup – the top set of ball bearings are held inside this cup.

Top or head race – this is the part that is press-fitted into the frame and retains the bearings onto the head tube.

Crown race cup – again this is press-fitted into the frame and holds the lower bearings inside.

Crown race (under) – this is press-fitted onto the fork crown and retains the bearings onto the fork, they are usually sealed to prevent water and dirt getting into the bearings.

on, but they have and I really think that they are change for change's sake, because they don't work any better than the standard cup variety and they also require the frame to be made with very exact tolerances. Altering this after the frame is constructed becomes very tricky.

Bianchi's benchmark Specialissima frame once used a similar system back in the 1950s but they stopped using it. I suggest that this was because the cups inside the head tube wore out and pitted quickly and the available spare head parts and bearings weren't really very good. Needless to say Fausto Coppi's bike still hangs on the wall at the Bianchi factory, with the integrated unit intact, but since then frame builders have gone down the route of using individual and replaceable headset parts.

Nowadays manufacturers of aluminium frames often use integrated headsets and they suggest that this is to make them stiffer and lighter than a standard head tube arrangement. In my opinion this is unproven and, although shorter, slimmer head tubes generally put more strain on the bearings than longer fatter ones, this is a questionable departure from a system that works very well and is easily maintained.

Early integrated headsets, especially in titanium frames, created a hell of a problem for bike mechanics, particularly because titanium is a tough material. Delicate bearing races do not like being forced into place, especially into a material like titanium that can't easily be worked or properly prepared with hand-operated workshop cutting tools. Manufacturers who use integrated units also say that it improves handling and steering characteristics. This is nonsense and is more likely to be a way of keeping the frame and fork a complete unit. Although the integrated headset looks burly and beefy and can be sculpted into some pretty beautiful shapes, it has little to do with function, serviceability and component choice – that is the beginning and end of it in my view. It is style over substance.

Chris King

2801 NW Nela Street
Portland
OR 97210
USA
www.chrisking.com
+1 800 523 6008

I have very few components that have lasted well over 20 years (although one that immediately springs to mind is a Campagnolo Record double-bolt seatpin that is seized into my hack bike). But the one that certainly never fails to amaze me is a 2.5cm (1in) Chris King Aheadset. It's been in more bikes than I can remember, including (originally) a Bontrager mountain bike, a Chris Dekerf road bike, numerous cyclo-cross bikes and a Bianchi track bike. Latterly it resides in a Pinarello Sestriere road training frame, a current favourite bike on which I do all my winter miles. And it's still as good as new.

Very few small independent manufacturers can claim to have made components for both Tour de France winners and Mountain Bike World Cup winners alike. Chris King is one of them, such is the trust placed in his work and this simple component. So what is all the fuss about? Well Chris King is an engineer who has also built custom frames. He designed the first sealed bearing headset in 1976 and from then on that's all he did, for many years. He perfected his product, which is the 'secret' behind the current range of Chris King headsets and Aheadsets. His obsessional attention to the details of this component and the tolerances under which they are manufactured is unique. Unlike many head parts, which use preparatory bearing fittings or off-the-shelf cartridge units, Chris King bearings are designed specifically for the task in hand.

Over the years I have had numerous Campagnolo, Shimano, Stronglight, Mavic and Edco headsets and Aheadsets, some good and some not so. I have even had headset bearings fail after a few weeks' use. But my King headset is as smooth as it was the day I bought it and, most importantly, it has outlasted frames, even the ones that have been crashed and thrashed.

'He designed the first sealed bearing headset in 1976 and from then on that's all he did, for many years.'

Wheels

The Right Wheels for You

Wheel choice is a big subject. Wheels are very personal – everyone makes different demands of them, and they often need to be custom built to suit the rider and the style of riding for which the bike is intended. The standard set-up on a road bike will be 32-spoked hubs laced into single- or double-eyeleted rims with stainless steel double-butted spokes. Many wheel builders have different opinions and techniques when it comes to the final build, but the standard wheel is a wonderful bit of engineering and, when built well, will outlast the components it is made of. However, good wheels are not just good components laced together – they need to be assembled correctly.

Wheel builders have the best experience of what makes a good wheel and they all have a variety of special skills that can never be replicated by a machine. Wheel builders are more accurate and take more care in the truing process and, like frame builders, they will inspect and choose the appropriate components for your requirements.

Many riders are obsessed with the latest and lightest wheels, so they may fail to notice the consideration that wheel builders and designers put into their craft. Second to building the frame the wheel build is the most involved process on a bicycle. For this reason handmade wheels are the best, because the truing, dishing (the offset, especially noticeable in a rear wheel, that ensures the rim is central to the forks or the rear triangle) and balancing process requires experience and a good eye. Handmade wheels are also often the longest-lasting option.

Lightweight Wheels

There is a convincing argument that light wheels are a good idea. Professional riders love light wheels and often they try to get the most advantage from their wheels by using lightweight tyres on the most expensive high-tech wheels available. But (and it's a big but) if they wreck a wheel or have a puncture they will simply get a new wheel from their team car. Without this support you may well have to consider budget constraints when buying; if you want your wheels to last a few seasons then lightweight might not be the best route.

Light wheels have great benefits for the rider. Not only do they save overall weight, they also accelerate quickly and can offer a more responsive ride. However, spare a thought for the hand-built wheel – with care in component choices you can build a pair that will compete easily with the weight of a more expensive complete wheelset and, if they are built well you could easily have a set that will last longer and run truer than a factory-built pair. When used on a daily basis, expensive wheels are less likely to be hardwearing and will soon deteriorate as the individual components are pushed to the limits of material technology. Save them for best – for race days and sunny summer rides. Training rides in the rain and in wintry conditions will reduce their life considerably.

WEIGHTS

The weight of a set of 'standard' 32-hole wheels isn't that much heavier than the more expensive options made by the wheel manufacturers. They can cost a lot less too, sometimes even a third of the price of a set built by a wheelset manufacturer. I think that a set of hand-built wheels is best for everyday use, especially when aerodynamics and rolling resistance will be less of an issue.

Standard hand-built*:
32H Campagnolo Record hubs
DT spokes
DT RR1.1 double-eyeleted rims:
1750g

Race hand-built*:
28 Hole DT Swiss Ceramic bearing hubs
DT Revolution spokes
DT RR1.1 single-eyeleted rims:
1391g

Wheelsets*:
Campagnolo Bora: **1325g**
Shimano Dura-Ace WH-7850-C24-CL: **1392g**
Mavic Carbone SL: **1765g**
Lightweight Ventoux: **990g**

*All weights are based on manufacturers' information.

Track Hubs

Track nuts 15mm (⅝in)

Lockring

Sprocket threads

Flange

Hub body

Flange

Cone

Lock nut

Track nuts 15mm (⅝in)

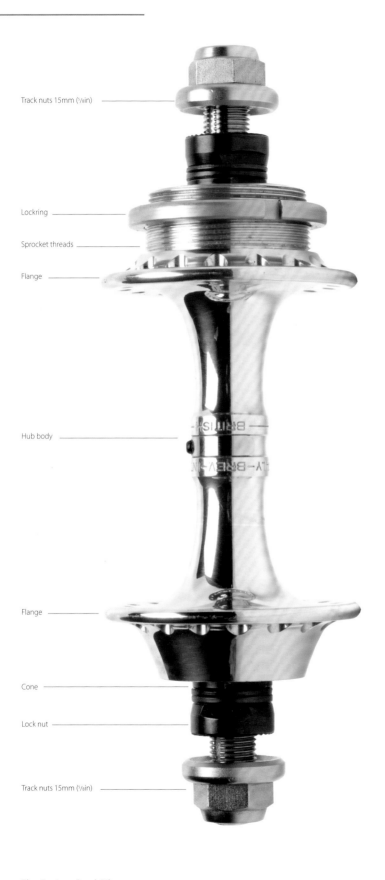

'I adore the simple beauty of the track wheel. It's perfect and is perhaps the finest combination of wheel design, physics and bicycle wheel aesthetics.'

Single speed hubs

Single speed and track wheels have a distinct advantage over geared road wheels in that they are far stronger and less likely to break spokes, and the hub is narrower than a standard road wheel – 120mm (4½ins), as opposed to 130mm (5ins) for a derailleur-geared bike – so there is more symmetry in the spoke tension and the shorter axle is stronger. The result is an almost indestructible wheel.

The hub has two threads on the drive side: the sprocket is a right-hand thread and tightens as you pedal; the lockring is attached via a slightly smaller left-hand threaded section – when tightened up against the sprocket it prevents it coming undone. Some experienced track riders remove the lockring completely from the rear hub. This allows the sprocket to spin off should the chain come off suddenly and get tangled, which could cause a nasty accident. However, lockrings are recommended for road use as they allow for safe back pedal braking on long descents.

Track hubs can be single or double sided. As you can swap the wheel around with the double-sided variety, they are preferable when using two sprockets for road use or when using a single freewheel on one side.

Buy a decent sprocket – Campagnolo, Phil Wood and Shimano are expensive but worth it, as cheap pressed cogs aren't round and can lead to tight spots in the pedalling action which can wear out your chain and chainrings quickly.

Road Fixed

Gears and brakes need regular cleaning and putting in plenty of miles in the winter is bad for your bike. Chains and cassettes wear out at an alarming rate in bad weather and cleaning off a couple of months of gear goo from your chain can take up considerable time. So road fixed single-gear bikes are a great idea, for commuting especially. You don't really need big gears in the winter as how fast should you be riding anyway? And the faster cadence needed is good for you – I'd suggest that there are few riders out there who would benefit from some pedalling lessons. Fixed-wheel road riding is hardly a new phenomenon, there was a time when all bike racers switched to a fixed for the winter months, and all pre-war Tour de Frances were ridden on a single speed. Although not really suited to the Alps, single-speed bikes are perfect for flatter regions and can be loads of fun. Winter training fixed gear bikes with mudguard eyes and braze-on fittings for racks and water bottles are rare, custom builders will build them to your requirements. 'Pure' track racing bikes tend to be a bit twitchy for road use and you can't get mudguards to fit or brakes front and rear for that matter – but the main problem with pure track bikes on the road is they aren't too comfortable for longer journeys and country road training. Fixed bikes are very much the fashion for city riding, and they are well suited to short distance commutes; however, two brakes should always be used and you should never ride a bike on the road with no brakes. It's not cool.

Fixed riding has the great advantage of maintaining momentum, which is one of the reasons it is sometimes favoured by time triallists and for specialist hill climb events. Your pedalling action will become very smooth (the French call this *souplesse*), which is why track riders always have a good pedalling action. After thousands of kilometres you will begin to use more of the pedal stroke to get the power down. The climbing technique is also useful as a single gear means you have to get up the hill in the only gear you have. It stops you getting lazy and using the gears, but it also teaches you how to squeeze every bit of advantage out of your climbing technique. Fixed can also add another dimension to riding in the wet or in slippery conditions, and offers better balance and speed control than a freewheel bike. This is one of the advantages of riding a fixed in the snow or ice.

A single freewheel is not a soft option (although die-hard fixers won't agree). It has all the simple benefits of fixed but the ability to freewheel down hills is an advantage, especially if you want to keep up with the pace when training in a group of riders in the hills.

Frame

Ideally, go for a frame with track style (horizontal, rear facing) rear fork ends and 120mm (4¾in) track hub rear fork end spacing. You can buy a fixed hub converter for 130mm (5in) spaced Shimano road hubs (Surly make this, it's called a Fixxer) or, if you want freewheel only, try a single-speed converter, which allows for spacing an 8- or 9-speed freehub body for single gear use. SRAM now make a rear hub that will fit a standard road bike spacing and can be switched with a screwdriver between fixed and freewheel. For fixed road frame conversions make sure you use a hub with nuts rather than a road hub with a quick-release skewer. Threaded nuts will hold the chain tension far longer than a skewer, which can slip under power.

If you have an old steel frame you could consider having it renovated and returned to the road as a single speeder. This can be expensive but if the bike is in good condition and made from decent materials (for example Reynolds 531) it could easily be 'fixed'. Many frame builders offer this service. If you are riding fixed, check that the frame will allow for pedal overlap (so that your feet don't foul on the front wheel when turning at slow speeds).

Gears

Use a 42 x 16 if you live in a flat area, 42 x 18 if it's hilly. I know some people push bigger gears but it's better to learn to 'spin' than get bogged down in massive ratios. Even with 42 x 18 on the flat you'll be able to cruise easily at 32/35kph (20/22mph) if you are riding in a group, but will go a bit out of control, especially on descents, after that. Ride a freewheel at first, unless you have experience of riding fixed. The chain rolls over large sprockets and chainwheels more smoothly than it does over smaller ones. Larger sprockets seem to hold the chain better and don't wear out so fast – 44 x 20 is quite a good combination for all-round fixed use. Always use a ⅛in chain (wider than a ³⁄₃₂in derailleur chain) – if you use a single chainring check the chain tension regularly. Beefier chains stay put if the chainline wobbles a bit over bumps or when pedalling fast.

Chainline and tension

Chainline and tension are of paramount importance – buying a single chainwheel crank (Miche, TA, Campagnolo, Shimano and SRAM all do track cranks) and a suitably matched bottom bracket is the best way to get the chainline accurate. Although good ones are expensive, you will save the time it would take to get a standard double bottom bracket and old crank to work. You can change the chainring bolts to shorter ones on a double and ditch the outer ring. However, you must line up the chain so that the sprocket is directly behind the chainring. This is especially important if you are riding fixed as the chain will unship if the chainline is wrong. Chain tension is also important. Vertical dropouts don't work so well with single speed as you cannot move the wheel fore and aft, and the correct chain tension takes time to get right. It should rotate freely but not bow under its own weight. You can buy wheel tension devices that attach to the rear fork ends and take up the slack – although they work very well they look untidy.

Above Fixed track cog – get your gearing right for you, not the trend.
Right Paul Components track rear hub

Road Hubs

Bicycle hubs have been through a huge change in the past 20 years. Adding extra sprockets to the rear wheel has meant that the drive system has had increasing demands placed upon it, many of which have influenced the rear wheel's integrity and the overall strength of the bicycle wheel.

Originally the rear hub was a threaded unit that allowed a separate freewheel block to be screwed into place. This meant that the axle protruded, unlike the axle in previous single-speed gear hubs, hanging and unsupported by bearings at the locking nut end and away from the side of the hub body. The result was a weak point and the constant twisting of the drive side sometimes resulted in bent or broken axles. During the 1980s, as we moved towards seven and eight speeds, something had to be done to prevent breakages in the rear wheel, especially as the mountain bike placed new demands on the strength of cycling components.

More room was needed for more gear sprockets at the rear, which made manufacturers move the hub flanges closer together, and it became increasingly difficult to build a rear wheel that 'stood'. Rims were redesigned and strengthened and the hubs became the weakest point of the wheel, although broken spokes became a bigger issue too as higher tensions were required to allow for the increased dish needed in the drive side of the rear wheel.

Helicomatic

The flawed but inspired Helicomatic system, by French manufacturers Maillard, had facilitated easy changing of sprockets with a helix-shaped slotted cassette carrier that was integral to the rear hub assembly. Now there was no need for threaded freewheels and ratios could be swapped without huge spanners and easily damaged removal tools. It was a great idea but poorly executed. Shimano took their basic design idea and created the system that all racing bikes use today.

Hollow hub axle – quick-release road hubs all have a hollow axle to allow for the quick release lever shaft to pass through the centre of the hub.

Bearing position – on a rear wheel the bearings are placed as far apart as possible to retain a strong and solid platform for drive.

Flanges – strong flanges are needed to brace the spokes and they are spaced to allow the spokes to clear the cassette sprockets and retain the structural integrity of the wheel.

Hub body – the best hubs are made from single forged or machined pieces, keeping weight down and strength high.

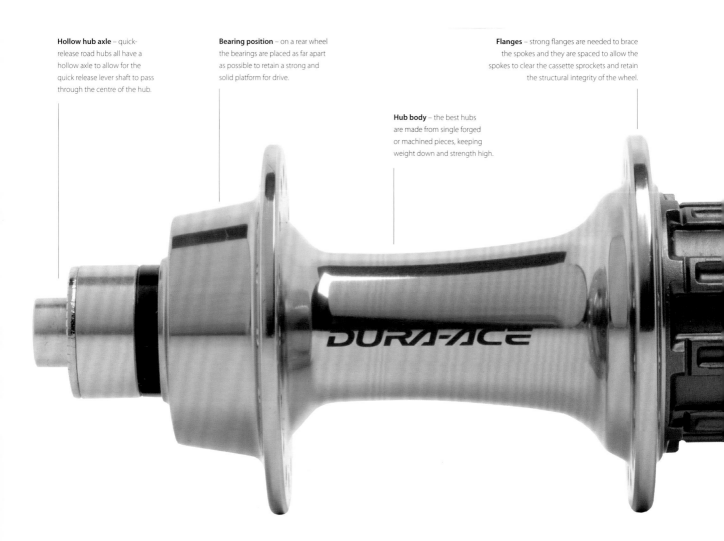

Shimano

Shimano realized that Maillard's design principle could solve the bent axle issue, because the bearings could be moved to the end of the axle, thus strengthening the wheel. The result was the Uniglide system, followed soon afterwards by their HG (Hyperglide) cassette hub system. It was better because it used larger bearings than the Helicomatic and the slotted cassette carrier was replaceable, so the freewheel could be kept spinning and the bearings could be regreased or replaced easily. The 'glide' part of the name referred to the altered shape of the sprockets, which facilitated smoother gear shifts (see also Cassettes, page 200). The entire system was designed in true Shimano tradition – for complete integration. On a practical level it was very easy to replace broken spokes, and you could build up a cassette from single sprockets – so for the gearing obsessed, it was a revelation.

Spoke holes – well finished and positioned spoke holes make building wheels easier and countersunk smooth edges (like these) also prevent spokes from breaking at the elbow.

Freehub body or cassette carrier – the slots locate on the inside of the cassette and patterns differ between the brands, the freewheel mechanism is housed inside it.

Campagnolo

Campagnolo were way behind their Japanese counterparts in hub developments, although in my opinion their Super Record and C Record hubs are some of the most beautiful bicycle components they ever made, especially the elegant and sculptural large flange 'Sheriff Star' Record C hub, which was also made into track configuration (and now fetches huge prices on eBay). However, Campagnolo eventually realized that Shimano had the right idea and they followed them into the cassette hub market with their 8-speed cassette hub. It wasn't as well conceived as Shimano's at first, being heavier and bulkier, so they made several modifications to bring it up to scratch.

There are now two distinct hub patterns, with either Shimano or Campagnolo compatible cassette carriers. The spline configuration determines which gear system you will prefer. The unsupported side of the hub is the part that carries the cassette, the group or cluster of up to 11 sprockets with a large variety of gearing configurations. So whose hub system is best? I have no preference, although the bearing quality in Shimano's Dura-Ace hubs is superb, and although the spoke holes are a little small, they build into a really special wheel. However, for me, the best generation of cassette hubs was the Record, from Campagnolo's original 10-speed groupset. These silver anodized hubs featured fully adjustable and replaceable bearings, complete with their signature oil hole and spring-clip cover. Their quick-release lever of this generation was one of the best they made.

Finally, SRAM cassette users can make use of Shimano-, but not Campagnolo-compatible hubs. This has had an influence on the popularity of the Shimano system, which is much closer to becoming the industry standard.

Right Campagnolo C Record cassette hub.
Far right Campagnolo front track hub with solid spindle.

Phil Wood and Royce hubs

Many quality hub-makers opted for cartridge bearings rather than the adjustable cup and cone style hubs from Shimano and Campagnolo. Those made by Phil Wood and Royce are some of the best I have used that don't have the loose bearing cone system perfected by Campagnolo and Shimano.

The beauty of these hubs is that they have fewer component parts and require less adjustment and servicing than standard cup and cone bearings. Once the bearing is push-fitted into the hub, the axle is pushed tightly into the bearings, then it's all kept in place with a single lock nut. This gives an instant smooth spinning wheel, as there is less possibility of the over-tightening that can occur in loose bearing hubs with poorly adjusted lock nuts and cones.

These hubs use readily available engineering standard 'sealed' or cartridge bearings. These are pre-manufactured units with the bearings that slot into a hardened steel cartridge, packed with grease and 'sealed' (although not completely waterproofed) with a plastic or labyrinth seal. They then press-fit into the hub's shell or cassette body. Nowadays they can even be Teflon sealed for added weather protection and, for the weight and performance obsessed, existing steel races can be replaced with complete ceramic bearing units if you wish.

However, despite the obvious advantages of simple cartridge bearing hubs, remember that they are only as good as the quality of bearings and standard of engineering of the hub shells. So shop wisely, as good-quality hubs can be built into fresh rims and expensive cartridge bearing hubs last much, much longer than cheap ones.

Top Phil Wood front track hub.
Right Royce rear cassette hub.

Tyres and Tubulars

As with saddles, shoes or bar tape you will have your favourite racing tyres. Fortunately, it's a very competitive market with several manufacturers making excellent products, so road cyclists are spoilt for choice.

Clincher tyres

The high pressure or clincher tyre has improved greatly over the past decade. A separate inner tube placed inside a lightweight has made riding a performance road bike a much more user-friendly experience. There are various tyre measurements and dimensions and each manufacturer has their own very different design, some with higher profiles or rounder-shaped carcasses.

Where you live and ride will have a large bearing on what tyre you use. Handmade tyres with file treads and super-thin sidewalls are lovely on the summer roads, but not so long-lasting in the deep winter. Rubber compounds also vary between manufacturers and this has the greatest influence on tyre choice. Some tyres cut up more than others and some grip better in certain conditions.

It never ceases to amaze me how many riders will spend a fortune on quality wheels and then throw on a pair of cheap tyres. Nothing can negate wheel performance more quickly than a pair of stiff, wooden-feeling tyres with an inflexible side wall and heavy bead. Supple tyres improve the handling of the bike considerably, so match the quality of the wheel with a good set of tyres.

A riding friend of mine once said that 90 per cent of punctures happen in the last 10 per cent of a tyre's usable life, which is true, but discovering when this stage in the life of a tyre will be reached is usually a process of trial and error. You'll usually get more flats in wet weather, especially after a period of dry weather – there is more gravel around to get washed into the road. I would usually expect to get 3,000–5,000k (2,000–3,000 miles) from a set of racing tyres in normal conditions.

Some riders ride their tyres into the ground. Not only will this mean you're waiting for them to fix flats all the time on the club run, but it also means they are putting their safety and yours on the line. Tyres should be replaced regularly and the benefits of fresh rubber should not be underestimated.

From left to right Race-proven tyres and tubular, Continental's Grand Prix, Vredstein's Fortezza tubular and Michelin's Pro Race 3.

VREDESTEIN *handmade* FORTEZZA PRO TriComp

SIZE 23-28" MAX 11 BAR (160 PSI)

MICHELIN PRO 3 Race ser

Fat Tyres or Thin?

Larger riders need larger tyres – weight, height and riding style will all have an influence on your tyre preference. Lighter riders can run narrower tyres at higher pressures, whereas heavier riders would find this uncomfortable. Reducing the pressure improves grip and comfort, but it also makes it more likely

that you will get impact punctures. Hot smooth roads can demand less from a tyre and lightweight tyres at high pressures feel fantastic. However, in the wet more grip is essential – this can be achieved by increasing the tyre size and reducing the pressure slightly, but this usually only really applies to racing on tubular tyres.

There are many theories of aerodynamics and acceleration with wider tyres, but comfort on longer rides is a much greater factor (and a lot more difficult to achieve). Wider tyres also offer a little more overall height to the bike, thus giving better pedal clearance for faster cornering. Wider tyres ride better and, as a result, tyre manufacturers are starting to make more slightly fatter 24mm (⁹⁄₁₀in) and 25mm (1in) tyres for road riding and racing.

So why do professional riders use narrow 22mm (⁷⁄₈in) tubular tyres? In fact, they don't always, and tyres are, if anything, getting wider. But the main reason is air resistance – pro pelotons move at much higher speeds than amateur riders and this means they will try to gain every possible advantage, however small. They can also handle a bike better than the average cyclist and tend to weigh considerably less, so they can use narrower tyres at higher pressures.

Rolling resistance

If you want to break the world hour record on the track, don't use 28mm (1⅛in) touring tyres pumped up to 60 psi, and if you want to win Paris–Roubaix, don't use 19mm (⅔in)

silk track tubulars at 200 psi. But it's not that simple.

Wide tyres only roll better at the same inflation pressure, but narrow tyres can usually be inflated to higher pressures than wide tyres, as there is less material in the carcass to deform. In addition to this, narrow tyres have an advantage over wide ones at higher speeds, as they provide less frontal area and,

The variation in rim section depth means that the standard length inner tube valve isn't going to extend far enough out of the rim to enable inflation of the tyre. So all

clincher tyre inner tubes now come with a longer valve option. Presta valves come in standard 36mm or 40mm length for shallow rims and up to 60mm for deeper section rims. For even deeper rims you can, in some cases, replace the valve core and add an extension or alternatively and more simply add an extension tube to the standard valve and leave the valve open permanently for inflation. Tubular tyres usually come with a short valve stem and this is best replaced with a valve extension when using deep-section rims. Most good wheelsets supply the right length valve extension tubes when you purchase the wheels.

Left, top to bottom Various options balancing comfort, performance and durability. The Continental 4 Seasons has puncture protection and at 28mm (1⅛in) is a more comfortable tyre than a pure race tyre. The Schwalbe is fast and smooth. The Deda Tre Corsa RS is very much a race tyre – run it at 120psi and you'll fly.

therefore, less air resistance. This offset of aerodynamics is a harsher ride, which fatigues the rider and can slow you down.

Tyres flatten slightly under a load. This deflection in the tyre creates a flat contact area and at the same pressure, a wide tyre and a narrow tyre have the same contact area. A wide tyre is flattened over its width, while a narrow tyre has a slimmer but longer contact area. The result is that a more comfortable wider section tyre can be run at a lower pressure, yet have similar rolling resistance to a narrower, harder tyre. It's confusing and may even contradict 'logical' thinking. Tyre manufacturer Schwalbe have done considerable research in this area and explain the principle of rolling resistance very well: 'The flattened area can be considered as a counterweight to tyre rotation. Because of the longer flattened area of the narrow tyre, the wheel loses more of its "roundness" and produces more deformation during rotation. However, in the wide tyre, the radial length of the flattened area is shorter, making the tyre "rounder" and so it rolls better.'

Inner tubes

A standard butyl inner tube is pretty reliable and light in weight. Lighter tubes are available and they add less overall weight to the tyre set-up. Latex tubes are more flexible than butyl ones and they do seem to roll and accelerate faster. They also deform and resist sharp objects better but they are expensive and don't hold the pressure as well as butyl, so the pressure has to be topped up regularly.

Right Butyl tubes are standard, and the default choice for the majority of riders.

Tubular tyres

Whatever is said of the quality of high-pressure (or clincher) bicycle race tyres, you still can't beat the riding qualities of a tubular ('tub' or 'sew-up') tyre mounted onto a set of lightweight 'sprint' rimmed racing wheels. Tubular tyres have a long history in bike racing, where they were first used over 100 years ago. They have a simple, slightly crude, construction with the cotton tyre carcass sewn up around the inner tube. This is then glued to a concave rim, which makes them involved to service and replace but also allows for unique riding qualities. Silk is sometimes used in the carcass of expensive tubulars to add supple ride without adding any extra weight.

Unlike clincher tyres tubulars can be inflated up to 200 psi and still retain their integrity as the tube is stitched and encased in the tyre's carcass. Clinchers would blow off the rim at anything over 150 psi and would probably distort quite soon after 130 psi. These pressures are very high for general road riding. In any event, changing a tubular at the side of the road is problematic, which is why clinchers have become the preferred choice for club riders.

The recent trend for deep-section and lightweight carbon rims has meant that the tubular tyre is having its very own renaissance. It's mainly because it's very hard to make a good quality carbon clincher rim, but it's also because professional riders always ride tubular tyres – they are faster, more comfortable and much grippier in the wet. They have the added advantage of not slipping off in the event of a puncture, so riders can still control the bike in the event of a sudden flat (an essential feature if riding on the track or in a fast-moving peloton).

Greg Lemond famously won the World Road Race championship on a 'soft' tub, something that would have been impossible on a clincher tyre. A clincher tyre rolls dangerously when it is soft and can roll off the rim completely, which may result in a nasty crash and ruined rims. Tubulars rarely pinch puncture as they have no rim edge to get caught against, nor can the tube get snagged on spoke holes like its clincher counterpart, as it is protected and encased by the tyre's carcass.

The big drawback to tubular tyres is that they need to be properly glued to the rim and, while pro riders have a team car full of spare wheels, fixing a flat can mean a long walk home for amateurs – a very good reason for using clincher tyres.

Opposite A tubular tyre gives the best road feel (at a price).

TUB CEMENT

All professional team bike mechanics have their own favourite tubular tyre cement. Some rim manufacturers have a type of glue suitable to their product, so stick with their recommended brand (excuse the pun). Continental glue is very durable and reliable and easy to use as it dries quickly and completely evenly. Some carbon rims now recommend using a carbon specific tubular cement, so be sure to use it if it is required. Continental make cements for either aluminium or carbon rims.

Track

This is one event that demands the use of tubular tyres. Lightweight tubular tyres with silk carcasses are often preferred. Favourites for elite track riders are expensive and they don't last very many races. High-pressure tyres can be used for training and are often used on concrete and outdoor tracks.

Tubs:

Dugast Pista Silks and Continental's Sonderklasse

Tyres:

Deda Tre RS or lightweight Continental Tempo tyres

Time Trial

Time trials require high rolling speed, so grip and fast acceleration are less of a priority. Slick treads are popular and, because of the nature of aerodynamic wheelsets (deep-section rims and disc wheels), tubular tyres are often the number one choice for time trialling. In my experience narrow tubs aren't always quicker than standard 22mm (⅞in) ones, mainly because they give a less comfortable ride.

Tubs:

Continental Podium, Vittoria Crono, Schwalbe Ultremo

Tyres:

Deda Tre RS Corsa or Continental Grand Prix Supersonic

Cyclo-cross

Perhaps a subject for a book all in itself, tyre choice for cyclo-cross can change the way that your bike handles. Fatter tyres are definitely better for all-round off-road use, so racers usually use 35mm (1⅓in) and 38mm (1½in) tyres, although sand and mud require totally different treads and tyre profiles. It's very involved and sometimes mechanics and tyre makers will even cut bits off the tyres at the race to create special treads, if the conditions dictate. The tyres should usually be run at 50–70 psi, harder if the course is rocky and dry. Deep-section carbon rims are popular with cyclo-cross racers, so tubulars are particularly popular.

Tubs:

Dugast Typhoon or Rhino, Vittoria Cross Evo or Continental Cyclo-cross World Cup

Tyres:

Continental Schwalbe CX Pro Cyclo-Cross or Continental Cyclo-cross

Pavé

The usual trick for riding the cobbles is to ride with slightly softer tyres. Clincher tyres are not that great on the stones, so if you have to ride on high-pressure tyres opt for 25mm (1in), or even 28mm (1⅛in) section tyres. Pro racers use special pavé tyres for races such as Paris–Roubaix, where the road surface is more like a mountain bike course than a road race. Riders often order special tyres from small handmakers such as Dugast or FBM, who will make special tread patterns and carcasses that are larger and stronger than standard road tubs.

Tubs:

Dugast Paris Roubaix, Continental Competition 25mm (1in) or Vittoria Pavé

Tyres:

Schwalbe Ultremo 25mm (1in) or Continental GP 4000 25mm (1in)

Road

There is a preference for tyres and tubulars that are consistent performers in all weathers. For racing tyres look for grip and speed rather than long life. For training use a fast clincher tyre and stick with the same brand as much as you can. You will learn how the tyre handles in all conditions and how hard you can push it in racing situations.

Tubs:

Vittoria CX, Deda Elementi Olympico, Continental Sprinter or Competition

Tyres:

Michelin Pro Race 3, Continental Grand Prix, Vittoria Open Corsa Evo-CX and Schwalbe Ultremo

Clément
Clément
CRITERIUM SETA
CLÉMENT CRITERIUM SETA
COLLÉ MAIN
MUNDIAL '82
PISTA CS
SETA

Rims

When selecting a rim the rider has to define what type of wheel they are trying to achieve. Wheel builders tend to use the shallow box section variety, rather than deep-section aero rims, this is because these will achieve the best combination of low weight and ride quality. As a rule, deep-section rims that are used in complete wheelsets have fewer spokes, to keep the weight low and to give the rim a bit of radial comfort. Hence, a hand-built deep-section wheel with many spokes will not be very practical. Wheel builders will have their favourites and their advice is essential as they can tune the wheel according to your weight, riding preferences and budget. Look for double-eyeleted rims that hold the spokes onto the rims, anchored at the rim edge and inside the rim section, rather than single eyelets that are just riveted onto the rim edge. Depending on the manufacturer, eyelets are made from aluminium or stainless steel.

The road rim needs an accurate and smooth braking surface. One of the biggest improvements in braking efficiency came about when manufacturers realized that the anodizing that once covered the entire rim, including the braking surface, took time to wear off. The result was that these rims offered little braking purchase in the wet – the brake blocks simply slipped off the surface – so they had to be worn in to remove the hard anodizing and break through to the softer aluminium beneath, which would provide some friction.

Clincher rims have to have a slightly more complicated cross section. There is no doubt that clincher tyres are easier to use (see also Tyres, page 86), but the rims are much stiffer than tubular rims, and not as strong. The first clincher rims had very poor joins where the two ends of the rim hoop meet – these were either pinned and glued or just push-fitted together. There was always a small step on the braking surface that could make an annoying clunk when braking. Worse than that, they could fail, sometimes when they were being trued. Current clincher rims tend to be deeper in profile

From left to right Mavic Reflex tubular sprint rim, Mavic Open Pro clincher rim, Ambrosio Excellight clincher rim, Ambrosio Nemesis tubular sprint rim and DT RR1.1 clincher rim.

than tubular rims and the clincher rims of the past and they are now welded together to provide a strong join.

Tubular (or 'sprint') rims are the simplest rim shape. Tubular rims have a single box section and the eyelets pass through the rim to be anchored on the outside of the rim. The resulting rim is arguably stronger, yet more flexible, than a clincher rim. These rims are usually used for the cobbled classic races in France and Belgium in the springtime, mainly because the riders like the predictable, comfortable ride that these tubular rims offer but also because they will 'give' a little over the bigger stones and potholes. Arguably, combined with a wide heavyweight tubular tyre, this ability to absorb the big hits makes them less likely to puncture. Very few teams use deep-section rims as they transfer far more shock through to the handlebars. This is one of the reasons why I prefer a hand-built, 32-spoked, three-cross wheel for long-distance training rides and racing over rough road surfaces, built with either tubular or clincher rims, as these provide a more comfortable ride than most complete wheelsets and are definitely more serviceable.

Ambrosio make some wonderful rims for both tubular and clincher tyres. I have built with their rims for many years – they are consistently round and build into a solid wheel and I prefer the feel to the ride provided by their Excellence or Excellight SSC clincher rims. The Ambrosio Nemesis rim is still one of the most popular tubular rims at the cobbled Classics. Although it's fully anodized it has a flat braking surface and it is strong and quite light. Ambrosio still make the Montreal tubular rim, which was used by professional teams through the 1980s and 1990s. It lacks a decent braking surface but is well suited to track wheels and retro rebuilds. All top-quality Ambrosio rims are balanced by using a weighted cover over the valve hole, which counteracts the extra weight on the opposite side of the rim where the rim is joined. They use stainless-steel double eyelets and are deep anodized with laser-etched graphics, so they stay looking good for a long time.

Mavic have a long history in bike racing and were the first to perfect the use of aluminium for racing bicycle wheel rims. Their rims are always well constructed and lightweight and have an excellent braking surface that is machined onto the side of the rim. Their Reflex tubular rim, with their trademark machined and welded SUP rim join and UB milled braking surface, with strong double eyelets, is excellent. A pair of 36-hole Reflex tubular rims is the basis for a pretty indestructible racing wheel. Mavic pioneered some excellent rim developments for clincher tyres, culminating in the Open Pro SUP, which is one of the most popular rims with wheel builders.

'I prefer a hand-built, 32-spoked, three-cross wheel for long-distance training rides and racing over rough road surfaces'

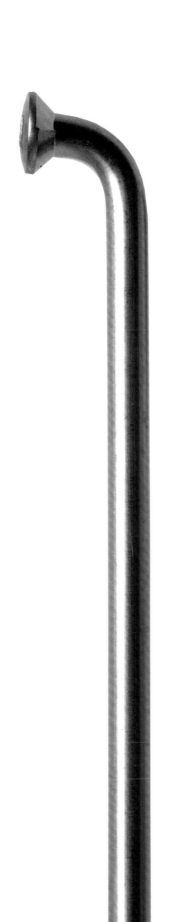

Spokes

Double-butted stainless-steel spokes were once quite an exotic addition to the bicycle wheel, but now they are the norm. Spokes were once chromed to add some shine to the bike, but many builders found them very brittle, and they were prone to rust. Developments have come and gone, with manufacturers experimenting with aluminium, titanium and even carbon fibre, but these have been dismissed by wheel builders, who recognize that stainless steel, with its strength, flexibility and corrosion resistance, is the most suitable spoke material.

Swiss wheel specialists DT make one of the best ranges of stainless-steel spokes available, along with Belgian company Sapim, who also make some very good lightweight spokes (their CX Ray is particularly nice). Aero spokes are popular with some of the specialist aero complete wheelsets, but they are expensive for hand builds, so my choice is always DT competition double-butted stainless-steel spokes, as they are light, strong and always consistently made. I always use brass nipples and only ever use alloy nipples for front wheels – in rear wheels alloy nipples can easily break under tension and, if left on a winter bike, they can easily corrode into the rim eyelets, making them impossible to true.

Left and right stainless steel spoke and brass spoke nipple.

Wheelsets

Complete wheelsets (where the wheel is supplied by a manufacturer as a readymade 'part') have been a regular fixture in the professional peloton for almost a decade. The first successful wheels in this market were made by Campagnolo. Their Shamal deep-section aluminium-rimmed wheels were released 15 years ago and used (on the flat stages) by Miguel Indurain to win the 1994 Tour de France. During the 1990s a variety of non-standard wheelsets appeared, even completely carbon-bladed wheels such as those made by American manufacturer Spinergy. Carbon disc wheels and tri-spokes had been used in time trials and track events but these were never an option for the road, where rider comfort and bike weight had a greater importance than aerodynamics. Complete wheels took a while to catch on with the discerning professional as the weight penalty was a problem when climbing the mountains and they just couldn't match the longevity of well-made hand-built wheels – some would say that they still can't. The early versions of the complete wheelset were very heavy and the performance advantage was negligible. These disadvantages were compounded by the fact that some had less lateral (side-to-side) stability, and those with a badly designed cross-section rim and too many spokes could also offer a harsh, unforgiving ride.

In 1995 the big news was that French component manufacturers Mavic were going to focus everything on the development of the wheelset. As Campagnolo and Shimano drifted away from wheel developments to focus on gear shifters, Mavic came up with some groundbreaking wheel developments. They improved their rims (now with machined and welded joins) and launched their first complete wheel, the Cosmic. This wheel was still fairly heavy, but the use of revolutionary straight pull linear spokes meant that the hub could be reshaped and the elbow of the spoke (the bend at the hub end, which was needed to hold the spoke into the hub spoke holes) eliminated. Mavic had realized that fewer spokes in a standard traditional pattern hand-built wheel often meant that the wheels had to be built with more spoke tension, therefore the wheel became more sensitive to spoke failure, usually at the elbow. Mavic's new straight spoke allowed for more tension and fewer breakages, and they could also add a wider aero cross-section spoke as it didn't need to be threaded through the small hole at the hub, which they also redesigned. As a result the Cosmic rolled well and looked the part, but the overall weight savings, with their aluminium deep-section rim were negligible.

Towards the end of the 1990s Mavic released the Helium, one of the first truly lightweight complete wheelsets, and it proved popular with professional riders, especially in the mountains. It was one of the first complete sets to weigh less than 2kg

Right Edge Composites' wheels – they have to be held to really appreciate the (lack of) weight

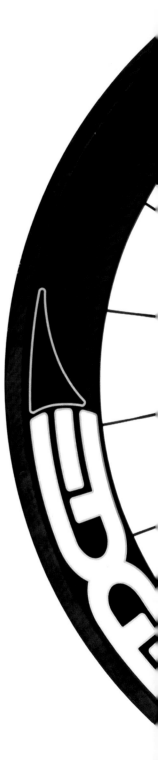

(4lbs 8oz). In actual fact it was around 1,500g (3lbs 3oz). Again, the problem was longevity, and if you weighed more than 80kg (176lb), you didn't expect to get very much service life from a pair. The standard profile tubular rim also meant that they were limited to racing and those who were used to gluing and preparing tubular tyres.

The good news for the road cycling consumer was that, as we turned the century, clincher tyre technology improved considerably, and this meant that the clincher tyre was taking over from the tubular as a satisfactory alternative for amateur racers. However, the shape of the clincher rim was limiting if you wanted to build the rim from carbon, so aluminium remained the popular, albeit heavier, material for clincher rims. Wheel manufacturers started removing even more spokes to save weight, but all this really did was weaken the structure and create problems when truing the wheels, especially when the spokes were held in extreme tension in groups of fewer spokes. What was needed was a lighter wheel rim held with more spokes, but providing less overall weight.

Mavic's Cosmic Carbone wheel was one of the first light-ish, deep-section carbon-rimmed aero wheels that rode fairly well. Launched into the professional peloton in 1997 it was a deep-section carbon wheel of sorts – but the rim was essentially a faring with the spokes attaching to a central standard shape rim. At this time very few wheel companies had mastered the art of a deep-section rim, in the traditional aluminium sense, where the aero section of the rim acted as a structural part of the wheel. Mavic's great success story for amateur riders was the Ksyrium aluminium wheelset, which used fatter spokes made from aluminium (so they could use fewer of them) and stronger and lighter aluminium rims. The result was a much better wheel than previous attempts, but, longevity-wise, it was still flawed. However, compared to all the other wheels around at the time, the Ksyrium was a huge step forward.

Spokes have often been the problem with keeping wheels spinning and their vulnerability has prompted wheelmakers to change specifications to beef up the construction and to improve the weak points identified by Mavic. Campagnolo took much of what Mavic had achieved with the Cosmic and redesigned their nipples to provide a firmer hold on the increasing spoke tension. They added concave washers and a domed end to the nipple, which improved the fit at the rim and allowed the spoke to find its perfect position when the wheel flexed. Their Neutron wheel introduced a really competitive wheelset into the market.

Finding a reliable carbon rim for high-pressure tyres is still a problem for manufacturers, although most have perfected all sorts of shape of carbon rim that can be built with fewer spokes at a higher tension. Improved brake pad compounds allow steady and sure braking in the wet. Opinions abound about the predictability of the carbon braking surface – some say that there have been more crashes in the wet since pro riders have been using carbon rims and that braking is less effective with the appropriate brake pads. However, this could have more to do with faster speeds and more riders in the bunch. Whatever the truth of the matter, there is no doubt that aluminium rims brake more predictably than their carbon counterparts.

Most of the professional teams have the option of a deep carbon rimmed wheel in their armoury. Why? Well they have obvious aerodynamic advantages but they also seem to roll better on the long, flatter (smoother-surfaced) races and can shave a little weight off a standard set-up, and the latest offerings can also climb, sprint and accelerate incredibly well. So many of the wheel manufacturers (Zipp, Shimano, Campagnolo, Fulcrum, Easton, FSA, HED, Bontrager, Rolf, Reynolds etc.) have a choice of several pairs in their ranges. They are expensive, but can now have spokes held securely at the rim edge (rather than just a 'faring' to an aluminium rim), improving the ride, increasing wheel life and reducing weight.

Perhaps it is because consumer demands are now very high that the wheelset market is such a huge part of the cycling market. A frame will last many seasons, but the wheel has an obsolescence factor and this means that your bike will need several sets in its lifetime. However, what wheelsets have really done is facilitate the development of performance for specific events and applications, where once only tweaks could be made to the standard wheel. These modern road wheelsets are all about performance, not training in the rain and off-road exploring, so be sensible with your choices and save the carbon for the summer.

Opposite Mavic has designed a very specific rim, hub, spoke configuration.

Mavic

Mavic's SSC (Special Services Courses) is the badge used to denote those products used by professional teams and the current range of Mavic wheels is the benchmark for performance wheels. The yellow Mavic-branded cars that follow the professional pelotons still offer service and neutral support to the riders, and replacing damaged or punctured wheels has been their expertise for decades. They have certainly benefitted from this association and concentrating specifically on the wheelset from 1995 onwards has given them a focus that few other companies can claim.

Mavic's Ksyrium wheelset has sold in its thousands of pairs, and it is still perhaps the most popular choice for users looking for performance matched with longevity and affordability. Recent modifications in their latest range-topping R-sys wheels have taken things a stage further by using composite materials in stiffer tubular section spokes and also in hub construction, which many of the other manufacturers using the standard wheel construction technique still haven't managed. They have also improve their rim technology with aluminium threaded nipples that screw directly into the rim. This opens the door to the next advance in tyre technology, where the tyres will be capable of being used without inner tubes on clincher rims that now have a sealed interior.

Carbon Sports Lightweight Wheels

German wheel-meisters Lightweight really grabbed the headlines when Jan Ullrich started using their complete 'monocoque' carbon deep-section wheels. He was followed by compatriot Eric Zabel, and Lightweight now support Team Milram. The Lightweight's construction is a little odd. Spoked yes, but also 'monocoque' in the sense that the wheel is constructed as one piece, as you would build a frame, with no possibility for adjustment for true or replacement of spokes. For a wheel builder it's a strange scenario, yet it also makes sense when you think about it – the frame cannot easily be adjusted for buckles so why should the wheels?

Lightweight's spoked wheels are handmade in Germany. They are built using the original processes and techniques developed by the wheels' inventors and carbon fibre wizards Dierl and Obermayer. When they started out it was a labour-intensive one-a-day process. They consist of an all-carbon rim with a lightweight foam core with a carbon fibre hub body fitted with DT-Swiss hub internals. The spokes are also made from carbon- and kevlar-threads.

Right Mavic's deep-section carbon rim and braking surface.

'Mavic's Cosmic Carbone wheel was one of the first light-ish, deep-section carbon-rimmed aero wheels that rode fairly well.'

The all-carbon standard rim is 19.5mm (¾in) wide and 52.8mm (2ins) high. As the wheels are mainly used in time trials and difficult mountain stages, such as those during the Tour de France, the carbon fibre braking surfaces provide adequate brake performance but they do need special compound pads to prevent erratic braking. The rim surface is sealed with a special clear coat lacquer and the wheels are without 'heavy' screws or spoke eyelets because the design allows the rim, spokes and hub to be laminated as one piece, forming an extremely stiff unit. This leads to a more trouble-free wheel that requires no maintenance. Now there is a shallower section Ventoux wheel for those looking for something a little less aerodynamic.

The spokes are incredibly tight and they ring like piano strings. The rim includes an integral magnet for your speedo and there's a microchip built into them that has all the wheel's build data stored on it for future reference.

Jan Ullrich and a couple of others used the 'uphill only' versions (I kid you not) in the Alpe d'Huez TT during the 2004 Tour and, although they still couldn't beat Lance (on much heavier Bonty's), the stage was set for their inclusion in many team's armouries. This uphill version is now available as the Obermeyer and is now, fortunately, capable of going down hills too. At around 1000g (2lb 4oz) a pair of Lightweights is the lightest complete wheelset on the market by a large margin.

The fact that they won't need truing is a huge plus for those who can't (or don't want to) use a spoke key. With the increasing popularity of wheelsets and the improved quality of rims, the need to carry out roadside repairs has decreased. I like the idea of being able to repair a wheel at the roadside but it's only going to happen a couple of times in a wheel's lifetime of cycling – such is the efficiency and strength of the well-made bike wheel.

The sprightly feel of a pair of Lightweight wheels does take a bit of getting used to – the combination of zero flex and maximum 'whip' is phenomenally effective. For me they are the only real alternative to a traditional spoked wheel as they offer real ride quality advantages, longevity and weight saving – huge improvements that many other set-ups can't match.

Right Lightweight by name…

Edge

Edge Composites are a specialist carbon manufacturer that started in 2005, but whose products have made an incredible impact in a relatively short space of time. Edge's engineers have worked for bike industry companies such as Schwinn/GT, Specialized, Felt, Reynolds and Easton. So engineering-wise, you're looking at over 30 years of carbon experience. Edge now employs 75 people and make all their products at their own plant in the Ogden, Utah, USA.

There was a time when Edge only developed tubes and component parts for other companies like Parlee, Independent Fabrications, Calfee, Vanilla, Crumpton and Rugamer. They are custom artisans who refuse to adopt the big box mentality.

Their rims are currently the most lightweight available for hand-building a quality performance wheel. Two of their best products are the sub 200g tubular climbing rim and 340g, 68mm-deep aero section rim, which are both designed without any rider weight limits. Where most very lightweight aluminium rims struggle to retain any real integrity, Edge have managed to make exceptionally strong rims and at a fraction of the weight of aluminium. But the big advantage is that their rims can be built into any wheel combination. So you are not limited to a standard hub and spoke combination; you can build a set to suit your preferences – though it does comes at a price.

Wheels and rims account for half of the company's production; they also make forks, handlebars and stems. Their forks in particular are popular in the discerning and slightly traditional world of cyclo-cross. And it is a sign of their confidence in their technology and engineering that they can make a product tough and responsive enough for the high demands of off-road riding.

Right Edge deep-section rim on a DT Swiss hub.

Quick-Release Skewers

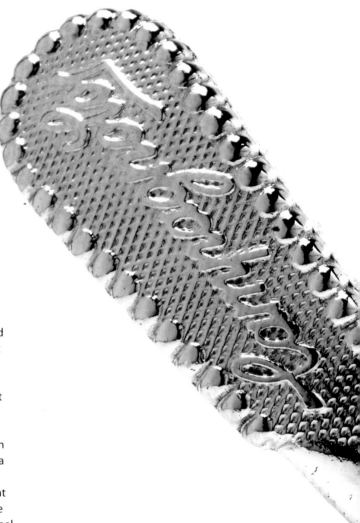

'Bisogno cambiá qualcossa de drio!'
'Something must change in the rear.'

It was November in the Dolomites. The day was cold and his fingers were frozen. After wrestling with his axle nuts and swearing at his flat rear tyre in the Gran Premio della Vittoria race of 1927, Tullio Campagnolo brainstormed an idea for the first significant improvement for the racing bicycle since the development of the pneumatic tyre some 30 years earlier. Tullio went home to his workshop in Vicenza with the idea that there had to be a quicker and easier way to change gear (the rear fixed wheel had to be swapped around to get a second gear) and to fix a flat. Three years later the legend of Campagnolo was born, as was the basic, yet ingenious, design for the quick-release skewer we still use today. It's something that we take for granted now, but it revolutionized the sport in the 1930s.

What set Campagnolo apart from many of the engineers of the time was that he was a racer and he loved cycling. So he spent time with the race mechanics and riders after he retired, talking about their needs and problems. This was a unique approach and he was constantly feeding information back to his workshop. But his big masterstroke was his endorsement of riders who used his prototype components to win all the great races. It was this determination and ability to carry out research and development himself, and in the field, that made Campagnolo what it is today.

Campagnolo's first quick-release lever was primitive, working on the principle of a cam-operated lever that was slotted through a hollow axle and threaded at one end. The first versions needed to be heavy duty as the gears were still fixed and this meant that the rear wheel had to be held very securely in the rear ends. The axles were much heavier in those days and the fact that the wheel was still symmetrical (as all double drive-sided wheels are) meant that axle breakages were rare. It was the development of the rear derailleur and the multiple-geared freewheel block that began a new breed of asymmetrical rear hubs and, with it, a new set of problems to occupy Sgr. Campagnolo.

The best quick releases are the ones that work in all weathers and in all situations. Many of the cheaper open-cam designs don't, especially in the wet when the plastic washers can fill up with road dirt and grit. The closed cam is the most practical, and professional mechanics always make sure that whatever wheels their team is endorsed by, they have a stock of these older but better quick releases on hand. Most of the bike is designed around the rider and this is the one thing that the mechanics touch, it's as if they have left a tool on each of their team's bikes.

'The best quick releases are the ones that work in all weathers and in all situations.'

Changing a wheel under pressure and in a race situation means that the spare wheels have to be prepared, the threaded locking nut set ready on all the spares at the correct distance to fit the dropouts and fork ends, so that the lever tension is perfect. The lever is always on the right-hand side of the bike, positioned parallel to the ground and tucked into the frame or forks, with the tips of the lever facing inwards, towards the bottom bracket. The forks will have the safety tabs filed off (not recommended if you want to keep your fork warranty) which allows the front wheel to be dropped in and out without having to readjust the locking nut.

The most skilled mechanics can change a rear wheel in a matter of seconds, so quick releases have to be reliable, consistent and solid. My preference is for the older, closed-cam versions that were made by Campagnolo and Shimano from the 1970s onwards. They are made from chromed steel and, although heavier, have the best lever action and the most comfortable levers. However, they aren't long enough for 10-speed rear hubs, so what levers should you choose?

Closed-cam quick-release skewers
The original design developed by Campagnolo has an internal mechanism that was cam-shaped at the end of the lever arm that pushes the lever locking nut shut. The all-steel parts meant that they were long-serving and easy to dismantle and service if they needed re-greasing.

Open-cam quick-release skewers
This is the only alternative to Campagnolo's original lever. These units are much simpler than the enclosed versions. They added the necessary cam shape onto the end of the lever, which means that the mechanism needs a bearing washer (usually made from nylon). This is placed on top of the locking washer that presses up against the dropout when the lever is closed. They are usually lighter than closed-cam mechanisms and, with fewer moving parts, are certainly a lot easier to manufacture. However, they do have to be made well – poor machine-made versions are unreliable and don't release as well as the closed-cam version.

Left to right Skewers from Campagnolo, Mavic, Shimano and Lightweight.

Campagnolo

The current Campagnolo Record quick release is a bit of a let-down, especially as Campagnolo invented the system, and their latest version is poor in function with little of the sculptural beauty of Tullio's first levers. The original 10-speed Record lever is my favourite quick-release skewer. With its aluminium locking nut with signature D-ring it is really easy to adjust and set up. The steel lever is comfortably shaped and easy to catch hold of, unlike many of the current skewers and, unfortunately, their own recent design 'improvement'. At 133g a pair the older Record skewer is hardly heavy – the latest Record lever is 120g a pair – and it's no surprise that team mechanics at the highest level still use this lever as their preferred tool for quick wheel changes.

Mavic

The French wheel manufacturers have taken a leaf from both systems and created a very usable skewer. The cam closing mechanism is made from steel and is covered with a plastic cowling to keep the grit away, so it's always smooth in operation. The lever is spring-loaded to aid undoing, although it can be quite stiff to undo if overtightened and the lever snaps shut, so perfect positioning is essential. In the latest versions the skewer shaft is made from titanium and the overall weight is low, around 100g per set.

Shimano

Shimano quick releases were lightened up and improved considerably during their boom development years, in the 1990s, when they were mainly associated with mountain bike groupsets. Like many of Shimano's parts they are very simple to use but are harder to service than the Campagnolo skewer, with sealed mechanisms that couldn't be dismantled easily. At 123g a pair they are light enough and work consistently.

Lightweight

Lightweight have opted for the open-cam design and have made a phenomenally lightweight skewer set that tips the scales at a scant 34g per set. They produced a minimal skewer with an aluminium shaft and titanium levers, which is the opposite of what many of the lightweight skewer makers do. They work surprisingly well and would save a bit of weight for a climbing bike. One drawback is that they are recommended for frames with vertical dropouts only, so how tight can they actually hold the wheel? They've passed German DIN tests (the major independent German engineering testing and safety institute) so presumably tight enough for safety's sake.

Bob Parlee

Parlee Cycles
119R Foster Street, Building 13
Peabody
MA 01960
USA
www.parleecycles.com
+1 978 977 7474

Bob Parlee is a composites expert. He worked in the ski business for a few years and then started working on boats. He designed centreboards and rudders, producing wing sections for use in the water in the same way that you would develop an airplane wing. This was for racing sailboats, Olympic class and America's Cup boats. In Essex, MA, where he lives, there is a long tradition of wooden boat building dating back to the 1800s and Bob is very capable with the traditional techniques, as well as the modern composites.

In working with carbon fibre and other high-tech fibres, Bob found an interesting juxtaposition with bicycles, especially time-trial frames and the boats he was making. He always enjoyed bikes and there were a lot of interesting bikes being built (this was in the 1990s before the UCI changed the rules), so that sparked the connection and ultimately led him into bike building. In 2000 he set out to build custom carbon fibre bicycles. The first sales for Parlee were in 2002, when Tyler Hamilton rode to second place at the Giro d'Italia on one of the first production bikes.

Since then, and in a remarkably short space of time, Parlee has built an excellent reputation for making very individual and custom-tuned frames. Unlike many carbon bikes Parlees are made using similar processes to those used to make lugged steel frames. They are assembled in a vertically standing frame jig using hand-mitred tubes, joined with hand-wrapped lugs – the main difference from the steel frame is that rather than being welded or brazed, they are heat-cured under pressure, using a unique process perfected by Bob Parlee.

The results are exceptionally lightweight frames that can be custom built to the customer's dimensions. The tubes can be selected, too, allowing the right amount of stiffness or flex, according to the rider's preference and desired weight of frame. Stock Parlees use unidirectional carbon tubes as standard, but optional upgrades include the super light SL tubeset, or an extra stiff XL tubeset and the X woven tubeset. Any combination of these tubes is possible, but Parlee will make every effort to ensure that the right tubes are used to get the desired blend of strength and rider comfort. Seat stays can also be selected, with either wishbone or more traditional looking straight stays (used on the Z1, shown here). These are a really nice touch in such a high-tech bike, adding simple, more traditional lines to the frame.

Their individual tube and lug construction (in many ways similar to the technique used by Colnago and Serotta) allows for a multitude of sizes, rather than a limited few out of single-sized moulds, which is how many of the mainstream offerings are produced. Best of all, if you crash a Parlee bike and

'The key is properly aligning the fibres.'

damage a frame tube it can be replaced, which until now has been impossible with the magic black material. There seem to be very few limitations to the customization available, just as long as it's carbon fibre.

Because of these groundbreaking, yet surprisingly traditional manufacturing techniques, Parlee are now one of the most respected carbon frame manufacturers out there – but they are not 'just' about engineering. With exquisite finishing and Bob's meticulous attention to detail they also have the look to match the performance. Among the current crop of carbon bikes I have ridden, they are some of the best performers available.

Materials used:
Exclusively carbon fibre for the 'frame' portion, but we use titanium and aluminium for various fittings and mounts where it makes sense. Moulding processes are getting more advanced, allowing for carbon to displace more and more metal each year, but there is still a need for some metal in frames, for example, where things are threaded in a frame.

Employees:
Approximately 12.

Price range:
US$3,400–9,200 for a frame set.

Waiting period (average!):
For customs, the average is 60 days.

Frames built per year:
Total, including our stock range(s), approximately 1,000.

Who are your customers and how would you 'define' them?
In general terms, our customers tend to be, like us, 'geeks' (but in a good way). They are mad about bikes. And there seem to be two distinct elements. Racers who want a great performing bike that will last more than a season and/or clients who simply love to ride, have been into bikes for a long time, have had lots of nice bikes and want to have 'the best' in carbon. Maybe they have a Sachs steel bike, an Eriksen Ti, a Pegoretti AL bike etc. and they want to have a benchmark carbon bike as well.

How long have you been building bikes?
Full-time, almost a decade now. We first sold Parlee-branded bikes in 2001.

Do you make (or have you made) frames for any professional riders or teams?
Yes, we have made many customs for pros (typically un-badged) and now we sponsor the UCI registered Fly V Australia team. They just did their first Tour of California, so it was exciting for us to see the team on TV here in the States.

What started your interest in bicycle engineering/design?
I always loved to ride. Loved touring all over the US in the 1970s, raced a bit in the 1980s and 1990s and just always had the bug. As a person who always built things, it was kind of a logical progression to do my own thing. Being exposed to composites in the 1980s and 1990s while I was in the boat business started to spark ideas in my mind. It always seemed to me that composites were going to be the future of bikes.

Who taught you to build?
Self-taught in regard to bikes, but a lot of what I learned in building windsurfers and boats was applicable to what I do now in bikes. I was able to work with some really smart composites guys in the early days who really helped me develop our custom moulding process, which is still unmatched for flexibility in geometry.

Who influences what you do now (if not all of the above)?
I look at a lot of modern art and industrial design. I am attracted to clean, elegant solutions to design and engineering problems, and try to keep all my bikes as 'clean' as possible.

What is the best material for frame manufacturing (and why)?
Carbon, not just for the obvious strength to weight properties, but also for the tuning options you get from manipulating the fibre composition and orientation. Most people still don't get this about carbon. You can make a bike as stiff as a board or as compliant as can be, just by changing fibre orientation.

How do you size your customers?
We have a pretty sophisticated CAD system that we built that can get a set-up dialled in within a millimetre or so. We try to work with shops around the world who have demonstrated fitting expertise so a client can work with someone locally and does not have to fly to Boston to get a Parlee.

What is the most exciting new development in frame design or tubing technology?
I think carbon is still the most exciting development. When you consider steel has been used in bicycles for over 100 years, carbon (and composites in general) is still in its infancy.

What's the most important element to the frame?
Again, the orientation of the fibres is what makes a bike great. In terms of individual sections, the chainstays are often overlooked or 'styled' to look 'beefy' or 'stout', and it really has more to do with the composition of the tube structure. Efficiency of fibre placement is really the key.

What do you want to achieve for your customers?
We want them to fall in love with the ride and feel that we took care of their bike as if it was our own.

Who is/was the best frame manufacturer or builder and why?
Impossible to say, as each process is so different. TIG in AL, TIG in Ti, lugged steel, TIG in steel, fillet-brazed steel, lugged carbon, tube-to-tube carbon, monocoque carbon…etc. All are so specialized; it seems that it would be impossible to have one 'best'. In terms of our unique process, our builder Rommel Mariano is incredible, the best ever.

'I was able to work with some really smart composites guys in the early days who really helped me develop our custom moulding process, which is still unmatched for flexibility in geometry.'

Bike Fit

Saddle, Fit and Position

'Men should never ride bicycles. Riding should be banned and outlawed.
It is the most irrational form of exercise I could ever bring to discussion.'

So said American urologist Dr Irwin Goldstein in 1997 after a big news story (based on his research) broke in the US press. It was about penile dysfunction and men becoming impotent as a result of cycling. The story spread through the world's press and was a huge blow to cycling. It was fuelled in part because Dr Goldstein whipped up the panic even further by claiming that around 100,000 men in the US would already be impotent as a result of cycling. Perhaps a more rational approach would be that the main issue with discomfort and the bicycle seat is that many people use the wrong saddle, wear the wrong clothing and have the saddle position set up badly. Don't women have just as many saddle-fit issues as men?

Fortunately, common sense has prevailed (professional cyclists do have children, after all) and although what Dr Goldstein said may have some basis in fact, the beneficial result for cyclists was extensive research by saddle manufacturers to root out the 'problem' with saddles. As a direct result saddle companies started designing all sorts of shapes of saddle, often with holes in the middle. This was something that many professional riders had been doing for many years (especially with leather saddles) to prevent pressure on saddle sores and boils during the Tour de France and similar long stage races. They would often cut away the sides of leather saddles, and many found that breaking in saddles on their training bikes was the only way to achieve the level of comfort a three-week stage race required. However, the problem I find with holes in saddles is that the opening has two sides to it and the holes themselves act as pressure points – so many people, me included, never got on with these either.

For me the 1980s was the seminal saddle decade and the saddles designed then are still very popular. These days Danilo Di Luca still uses a Selle San Marco Regal saddle, as does classics expert Tom Boonen. Lance Armstrong uses a re-badged Selle San Marco Concor and you still see the odd Selle San Marco Rolls or a Selle Italia Turbomatic in the professional peloton. Why? Because these saddles were designed for comfort and professionals have to sit on a saddle for the duration of the average working week. Because they are big, these older saddle designs absorb far more road shock. However, some manufacturers want us to buy state-of-the-art carbon fibre perches, but these offer little more than weight saving and not much in the way of comfort. So build up a bike with this type of saddle on and take a picture of it or hang it on the scales, but don't sit on it. Anything that looks like a razor blade is never going to be really comfortable – think of a G-string versus a pair of boxer shorts.

We now know that there are more physiological reasons for saddle discomfort. First and foremost you must ensure that your saddle is completely level and the saddle is at the correct height, which may mean getting a bike-fit technician to set you up properly. Make sure that you are in the right position and that the handlebars are at a suitable height to prevent you leaning too hard on sensitive body parts. An extreme riding position on a time-trial bike, for example, could

Opposite, top to bottom Fizik's Pavé and Arione, and Selle San Marco's classic but comfortable Regal and Rolls.

'First and foremost you must ensure that your saddle is completely level and the saddle is at the correct height, which may mean getting a bike-fit technician to set you up properly.'

cause problems as you are usually sitting further forward in the time trial 'tuck' and placing a lot of pressure on your perineum. So it is essential to get this part of the fit process done first. Good bike fitting will allow you to try out several saddles during the fitting process and some saddle manufacturers now let you try before you buy on loan saddles that retailers can arrange for you to test. It's well worth the time invested. I read recently that saddles are a 'contact point of personal preference'. While this may be an easy catch-phrase for product reviewers, it reflects the fact that we are all different and designs are changing to accommodate all bike riders, male and female.

So it is perhaps to some extent thanks to Dr Goldstein's claims that there are now many more saddle designs available, many with different widths to suit the variety of sit bone dimensions. And your sit bones are the first thing to consider when setting out to find your preferred saddle.

Left to right Fizik's Antares, Pavé and Arione – slightly different widths to suit different bones.

Seat Posts

The saddle is attached to the bicycle with a seat post, which is adjustable for saddle height and fore and aft positions according to the rider's preferred seating position. The shaft of the seat post is usually a tube that has a yoke or cradle at the top, secured to the saddle rails with either a single or twin bolt fixture, depending on the cradle design. Single-bolt seat posts, such as those made by Campagnolo, are easier to adjust, but two bolts always seem to be stronger and less likely to slip. However, either system works well if properly tightened to the manufacturers' recommended torque setting.

The diameter of the seat post has always been influenced by the thickness of the frame's seat tube. Thin-walled steel frames have historically usually used 27.2mm, 27mm or 26.8mm, although there are as many sizes as there are frame tube specifications (which dictates the post's diameter). Some early aluminium frames even opted for a smaller 25mm post, although as seat tube diameters have increased, especially with aluminium and carbon fibre frames, the larger 31.6mm diameter is popular, and some frames are even bigger. The bigger diameter tube has been popularized with sloping or compact frame designs. It looks more in proportion with fatter-tubed bikes and obviously adds strength and stiffness over the smaller diameter, especially when extended further from the frame. However, the most popular size nowadays is 27.2mm. Seat post lengths vary from around 200mm up to 450mm and they all have a minimum insertion point, usually about 70mm from the open end of the tube. However, the longer the seat post, the more of it there is to be secured into the seat tube.

The seat post is fixed into the frame with a seat post collar or clamp that simply squeezes it into the seat tube. However, on a lugged steel frame the seat post is usually clamped in place via a binder bolt that passes through the seat tube lug. All seat posts

(especially carbon ones) should be checked regularly at this insertion point as the slot in the frame can often be a source of compression damage to the post.

Many carbon monocoque frames now have integrated seat posts, where the seat tube extends past the top tube and thus removing the need for a separate seat post. These are limiting if you aren't certain of your saddle height and the seat tube usually needs to be cut to achieve the desired height. If you get this wrong you could have a very expensive mistake on your hands. It is claimed that integrated seat post frames are stiffer and lighter than frames using a standard adjustable seat post. I believe that this frame design is a fad and the limitations in adjustment outweigh the questionable advantages.

3T's in-line carbon-shafted Race-Team seat post

> *'I snapped a previously damaged carbon post once in a cyclo-cross race, and I never want to have to pluck shards of carbon from my inner thigh again.'*

LAYBACK SEAT POSTS

Setback, offset or layback is the travel allowed for the saddle to be clamped in place behind the shaft of the post. This will be defined by personal preference and fit characteristics. A rider with a longer femur or legs will usually opt for more layback. Layback can be anything from 2mm up to 50mm. Recognized manufacturers such as Campagnolo provide a standard 25mm of layback.

IN-LINE SEAT POSTS

Smaller riders may prefer to use an in-line seat post, where the saddle can be positioned further forward on the rails, as the cradle allows up to 25mm more of forward adjustment over the layback design. In-line posts are often preferred by track and time-trial riders, who need a more powerful position, forward of the bottom bracket, which allows them to exert more powerful pedal stroke. However, as with all fit issues, always ask a professional fit technician for advice on what is best for your physiology.

Right ProComponent's PLT aluminium seat post.

The Custom Road Bike

Materials

Carbon seat posts are the most popular for road bikes. They are light and extremely strong. However, choose your carbon post carefully and look after it, and if you are riding cyclo-cross consider a more serviceable material. I snapped a previously damaged carbon post once in a cyclo-cross race, and I never want to have to pluck shards of carbon from my inner thigh again. The abuse of carbon fibre components in cyclo-cross (the constant washing of dirty bikes and the extreme impacts of riding off road) makes carbon an unsuitable material for cyclo-cross bikes. Always keep a careful eye on your seat post – remove it and check it for signs of wear, especially any scratches and gouges that may develop into cracks and eventually lead to failure. Use carbon preparation compound (not grease) on the shaft to prevent it seizing into the seat tube.

Some manufacturers now make monocoque carbon posts, where the cradle is moulded into the shaft of the seat post. As with frames that have integrated seat posts these can be limited with regard to adjustment and should be used only if you are certain that they will be appropriate for your desired saddle height and position. They are also less likely to allow for a lot of layback.

Steel and titanium posts are available for riders looking for longevity and perhaps even a little extra comfort from a more compliant material (the inherent elasticity of steel and titanium posts can give them added flex). Aluminium is perhaps the best material for seat posts. Aluminium posts are usually solid and reliable and less likely to seize in a frame if properly prepared when the bike is assembled and, unlike carbon, they are not prone to catastrophic failure.

Right Carbon Campagnolo seat post and the (crucial) seat binder collar that the majority of frames will need.

Brooks Saddles

Downing Street
Smethwick
West Midlands B66 2PA
UK
www.brookssaddles.com
+44 121 565 2992

Brooks are one of the oldest manufacturers in cycling and their quality is the secret to their popularity. Their saddles aren't everyone's first choice, but they are truly handmade and perfectly finished. In the 1930s and 1940s Brooks were, pretty much, the exclusive saddle for the professional peloton. In 1936 Brooks happily pointed out that every single rider at the Tour de France had used one of their 'comfort' saddles.

The design and manufacture of cycle saddles has largely followed the pattern laid down by John Boultbee Brooks in 1866. Today, Brooks' leather is cut from hides sourced in Ireland and tanned in a specialist tannery in Belgium. However, the rest of the soaking, drying and forming process is done in the factory in Smethwick, Birmingham. The production of a Brooks saddle requires high levels of accuracy and attention to detail – it's a handmade item and many of the workers in the factory have over 20 years' experience.

The saddle uppers are blocked (shaped in male and female moulds) after the leather blanks have been soaked and partially dried. This preforms the upper of the saddle, which is then dried more thoroughly prior to being blocked again ready for cutting to final shape. Cutting the leather once formed in the mould is impossible for the beginner. It takes plenty of forearm strength and a technique developed by the cutters who can accurately skim the excess away, in the same way that a cheesemaker would cut a wedge. Using a frequently-sharpened American tool-steel blade, the craftsman trims the excess leather protruding from the edge of the blocking mould, leaving a shaped upper ready for patterning with the appropriate embossing stamp.

Like huge steam-driven presses from the Victorian age, mammoth specialist presses and spring coilers that occupy a good half of the factory rattle through miles of steel (and now titanium) section with ease to produce the rails and springs for the saddle chassis, which comprises a length of wire bent to form a pair of rails. At the rear the rails make a rigid join with a curved 'cantle' plate that stretches the width of the saddle. The nose of the leather upper is riveted to a narrower curved plate incorporating a Brooks-patented device that allows the upper to be tensioned, thus taking up any slack or sag that might develop over time.

Whether riveting the leather to the chassis by machine or by hand it is, it seems, a natural skill that you either have, or don't have – only a few workers at Brooks have perfected the technique. The checking procedure is rigorous. The slightest blemish in the leather will lead to the saddle being rejected,

therefore a careful thwack in just the right place is essential. The large copper rivets are effortlessly clouted into place and the smaller steel ones are machine-stamped into the cantle plates. They're all aligned by eye and there are remarkably few botches as the riveters fly through the daily inventory.

This process and much of the machinery and production techniques are the same as they were 100 years ago. The lasts that make the uppers are the same and the designs match those that were made in years gone by.

The stampings and nameplates are the same too. Keeping the branding just as it was appears to be as important as the quality that the factory strives for. All that has changed is the size of the range, the presentation of the product and the packaging, which now matches the quality of the saddles.

Brooks keep alight a significant flame for the original, groundbreaking designers of bicycles by doing a job you can't really do better with a machine. The beauty of a Brooks saddle is, undoubtedly, in the making. This is clearly a company that has stood the test of time.

Brooks, B17 saddle

Controls

Handlebars

Dropped handlebars are the recognized shape for road bikes. The standard road bar is usually 42cm wide, which (depending on the manufacturer) is measured from either the 'outsides' or between the 'centres' of each open end. Always use handlebars that match the width of your shoulders – they are available from 38cm to 48cm. The reach of the bar – where the levers sit on the curve of the bar – can vary from bar to bar by as much as 30mm, so make changes carefully, as a new set of bars can alter your position completely. Find the shape you like and then stick with it on all your bikes.

Generally speaking, narrower handlebars offer less leverage, but this is directly related to physiology and can be adapted to suit the branch of the sport that you do. Cyclo-cross needs more control for technical riding, so a wider bar that reacts quickly to direction changes can be favoured. Track racing, especially sprinting, needs a low frontal position with extremely strong bars, so steel deep drops are often preferred by track racers. There are different types of stem fitting size too – older handlebars come in a variety of sizes and they must be used with the recommended stem, although 25.4 mm (1in) is now the ISO standard size for road handlebar centre sleeves (the bit that the stem clamps onto). The 31.8mm (1¼in) 'oversize' bar is also very popular, and can match up well to the new oversized nature of frame tubes and fork blades.

Shapes for the curved part of the handlebar can differ greatly from one manufacturer to another and the traditional round-shaped bars usually come in shallow or deep drop. Road racers usually opt for a shallow drop, although longer armed or bigger riders (usually sprinters) will use a deep drop. If you find that you rarely ride on the drops, you may be using the wrong shaped bar.

ERGO BEND BARS

These bars have a flat section on the drop part of the bar and provide a more comfortable hand position than round bars. Careful installation of the brake levers is essential as the drop section of these bars has to be perfectly angled so that the fingers can still reach the brake and gear controls. Lever geometry has changed in the past couple of years to accommodate more bar shapes and allow easier access

Above Edge carbon handlebars.
Below Deda aluminium handlebars.

to the brake and gear levers. However, if you ride with the levers high on the bars the flatter sections can mean that your hands are too far away from the controls when sprinting on the drops. Every manufacturer has a variety of shapes to accommodate all hand sizes, and they also have a variety of drops (shallow or deep), so experiment and try out a few before you change bars.

INTEGRAL BARS AND STEMS

Many manufacturers have combined the bars and stem into one carbon-wrapped unit – notable examples are the Cinelli RAM and the Deda Alanera. I am not a big fan of these units for several reasons. First, they do not allow fine adjustment of the handlebar angle and, second, they are very expensive to replace. Interestingly, they are also heavier than a fairly standard set of aluminium bars and a separate stem. The same applies to carbon bars too, which offer little in performance advantage and are very susceptible to scratch damage at the clamping area by the stem when adjusted for angle. And, if they fail, it's usually pretty catastrophic.

CRASH DAMAGE

Carbon handlebars must also usually be replaced in the event of a crash and, depending on the scale of the impact, aluminium bars should also be carefully reviewed after crashing. The stem can be saved and the bars swapped, thus saving a lot of money. It's hard to see the full scale of the damage under wraps of bar tape, so please take great care inspecting the bars after mishaps – broken bars in race bunches or on alpine descents make for a very scary experience.

Top Deda Newton Oversize aluminium bar with a near-perfect drop.

Above The more experimental curve of the Edge carbon bars.

Opposite The Deda Newton handlebars securely held by the matching four-bolt stem , which spreads the clamping forces equally.

Aheadstems

There is a multitude of Aheadstem shapes and sizes. The original quill-stem design allowed for far more height adjustment. The only way to change quickly the height of the Aheadstem is to add spacers under it to lift the whole assembly higher on the fork steerer. However, if you have cut the steerer already this will be difficult. Alternative angles are available and you can flip the stem if the height is too low, although this can be very ugly. Oval Concepts offer a huge range of stem lengths and angles, including an adjustable stem that can be used to experiment with stem position.

Stem angles are now pretty limited. The manufacturers all quote different angle references, although an angle of 10° below the vertical now seems to be the most popular. If you want to raise the bars by a few centimetres without flipping the stem you can also use a 0° (zero rise) mountain bike-style stem, which can be found to fit oversize 31.8mm (1¼in) road bars.

Standard lengths are usually available from 50 to 150mm in length. Be careful, though, as over-long or -short stems can have a dramatic effect on the handling of the bike. I would suggest that anything under 90mm will make the steering noticeably twitchy, and anything over 130mm (5ins) will make it sluggish. Some professional riders like a neutral handling bike and a longer spread-out position and will therefore opt for a 140mm or even a 150mm stem, but in my experience it makes the bike very long and can alter the weight distribution, a result that is best reserved for those who know that it's exactly what they want. If you feel too stretched out on the bike then refer to the fitting section of this book (see page 118), but if the bike needs a short stem and is too high, or if it needs a long stem and the bars are too low, it's a sure sign that your bike is the wrong size. Women, however, may need to use much a shorter stem than men – the handling will be fine when combined with a smaller bike with corrected geometry.

My preferred stems are made from forged aluminium (like those made by Deda Elementi or Pro, shown here) and have four bolts in the clamp at the front of the stem, to retain the bars, and two at the fork steerer clamp, to hold the stem firmly to the fork steerer. Carbon stems may look the part (and are certainly very expensive), but they are usually made of aluminium with carbon wrapped over the top. The weight saving is minimal, usually 10–20g (⅓–¼oz), so they offer little in performance advantage.

Opposite, from top ProComponent PLT forged aluminium stem, Edge Composite carbon stem, Deda Elementi's forged and CNC-machined Newton 31.

TORQUE WRENCH

These days lightweight carbon stems and bars require careful setting up and adjustment. All manufacturers now supply recommended torque settings for bolts and clamps that hold the bars in place and the stem to the fork steerer. You must always use a torque wrench to adjust them and you must make sure that the gaps at the edges where the stem clamps the bar are evenly spaced. Pinching or angled gaps on the clamps can result in damage to the carbon and failure. Equally any scratches to the surface of the carbon may effect the integrity of the material. Be very careful and keep a close eye on the condition of the carbon.

Handlebar Tape

The former world pursuit champion and six-day star Tony Doyle would allegedly agonize over the wrap of his bars, and would have them re-done, even minutes before a pursuit heat, if they weren't quite perfect. Most professional riders are the same – bars need to be perfectly covered, clean and equal in every way possible. Staring at a gap in the wrap is not going to help your morale.

Prior to the 1980s the only tape available was simple cloth tape, which was not very comfortable. It lasted well and new tape was a once-a-year occasion, even for professionals. Then the colours in racing bicycles and team kit exploded, so the tape to use was Benotto. Its metallic cellophane appearance was certainly appealing, and it was the finishing touch that set a pro apart from the amateurs, who used cloth tape or, even worse, that horror of all handlebar horrors, sponge-tube shaped Grab-On.

However, as far as grip and cushioning is concerned, Benotto was completely useless. A combination of sweaty hands and Benotto tape would have you slipping off the bars in no time,

so a good pair of grippy gloves was essential. We didn't care. If it was good enough for Hinault *et al.*, it was good enough for us. Better still, being cheap, it was the one thing you could afford to experiment with and still have your bike looking 'pro'. The myriad colours meant that you could even colour-code your bars and turbo saddle, even if the colour was fluorescent green.

Benotto tape died off when bar controls had to be taped onto (and under) the handlebar tape. Cushioning became popular, so Benotto ribbon was as good as redundant. In 1986 Cinelli launched a luxury feel cork ribbon – it had a foam texture with added flecks of cork and it made the handlebars a joy to hold, especially on the cobblestones of Flanders and Roubaix. It is still made today, a testament to its popularity.

Nowadays handlebar tape comes in a multitude of different textures, thicknesses and finishes, so experiment with different makes, especially as it's relatively inexpensive. New tape makes a big difference to a newly cleaned bike – you will never see a pro racer with dirty tape.

Brooks leather tape (with sticky-backed tape underneath) is new, although it adds a classic appearance to a bike and lasts very well, improving with age. It's available in a range of subtle colours.

WHITE OR NOT

Bar tape is a very personal choice and therefore there are a host of different colours. Colour, in my view, should be as neutral as possible so white and black are my preferences. But if you fancy a splash of colour then matching bar tape with saddle colour is usually a good start, trying to match the paint on your bike isn't always a great idea, not quite matching can look terrible. But whatever colour or make of tape you go for – practice applying it and get the wrap right.

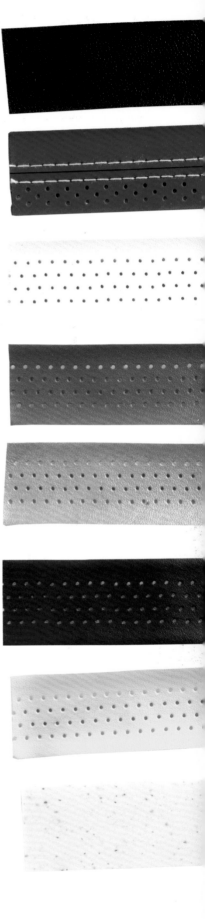

Right Bar tape options and colours are endless. Newer variants offer layers of shock-absorbing gel to insert under the tape but the standard offerings work for most applications and come at a price that allows fresh tape to go on as often as wear, tear and fashion dictates.

Brake Levers and Gear Shifters

Integrated brake and gear levers has been the biggest and best evolution for cycling technology, certainly in the last 20 years, but perhaps even longer. Gear shift and braking capable of being done from one lever has taken a long time to be sorted, and there have been countless variations on the theme. But now there are three excellent alternatives from Shimano, SRAM and Campagnolo. Getting to this point, however, has taken over 20 years of development and constant revisions. The quest to add more quality and more features to the bicycle is not always a bad thing. Bikes are better than they have ever been, and the race to find that extra sprocket has played a big part in the improvement in gear shifting.

During the 1980s the big manufacturers had toyed with the one click-one shift index system and had added more sprockets to the rear gear clusters. Shimano's SIS (Shimano Index Shifting) was very popular with a new breed of cyclist, especially during the boom years of the 1980s. For a decade or so, while many of the dyed-in-the-wool racers still made do with friction to hold their chains in the right gear, the all-Shimano equipped bikes were becoming lighter and more user-friendly than ever before. Campagnolo's response was the Syncro-Shift system, which was agricultural, to say the least, and their engineers seemed stuck with trying to adapt older, unsuited technology for a consumer who wanted slicker drivetrains and faster gear changes.

In 1990, yet again, Shimano redesigned the road cycling experience. They had already successfully dialled the index shifting experience, but STI (Shimano Total Integration) was a major development for racers looking for an edge. With the Dura-Ace 7400 series the Japanese giants stole a march on their Italian arch rivals Campagnolo. The idea of combining brake lever ergonomics with a faster, more instant shift proved a hard act to follow – the professional riders loved it and the European stranglehold on the road market began to shift to the Far East. After failing so badly at the mountain bike market perhaps Campagnolo had taken their eye off the ball, over-extending themselves into a market that they clearly couldn't improve upon. They buried themselves into reinventing their road groupsets, from the ground up. In 1992 the result was Ergopower, not as slick-shifting as Shimano's Dura-Ace STI, but with concealed cables and an index system that was a match for SIS and a considerable improvement on anything they had done previously.

The results from both manufacturers were astonishing. From a rider's point of view they allowed freedom to shift with minimal effort, to actually place their hands on the hoods in comfort and to be in complete control of the bike. At last they could shift and brake at the same time, saving valuable seconds and making for safer mountain descents and faster sprint finishes. Cycling had never been this easy.

INCOMPATIBLE?

It took Shimano many years to win at the Tour de France. In 1999 they finally did it with a Dura-Ace groupset, which was very advanced technically and designed completely around the rider–bike interface. The gears, the brakes, the pedals and even the chain had been considered as part of a complete component family. This was Shimano's main aim from the early days when they first launched Dura-Ace in 1973. Shimano's philosophy has always been for a totally integrated component groupset.

Nowadays that seems the norm, but in the 1970s the idea of having all your components from one manufacturer seemed bizarre. Back then you would build a bike from relatively compatible parts, often sourced from all over the world. The industry had standard sizes for most things (other than threads on frames) so French, British, Spanish, Italian and even Japanese components could all be on the same bike and work, after a fashion. The skill for mechanics was in adapting and modifying, which meant that they would need a workshop full of tools to build a bike from scratch. Nowadays, even the simplest bike needs just a few specialist tools and a couple of allen keys to keep it rolling along.

It's not a great thing that Campagnolo won't work with Shimano, and vice versa, and it means that careful consideration is needed when speccing a new bike (if all your wheels are Campagnolo then there's no point getting the latest SRAM Red groupset), but it does mean that if we buy into the compatibility ethos we get a great working bike – the Japanese–Italian bike parts race of the 1980s has made sure of that.

Campagnolo 11-Speed Ultra Shift

Next to the questionable one of an extra, eleventh sprocket, Campagnolo's biggest advantage over the opposition has always been multiple up- and down-shifting. Since the first Ergopower levers they have allowed for a sweep of the gear lever with your fingers to take the chain over several sprockets in one movement – the current 11-speed Ultra-Shift set-up will do five up-shifts at once. They use two separate mechanisms for this – a lever tucked behind the brake lever for the up-shift and a button on the inside of the lever hood for the down-shift. This button is activated with your thumb and you can do single shifts in one stab or multiple shifts with a sustained push – the current 11-speed set-up will now do three down shifts at once.

Ergopower was the first groupset from Campagnolo to use multiple gear selection as their shifting feature. It was the one advantage that down tube shift lever users had over the new converts to Shimano's STI system. They could still move through the whole range of gears in one shift, while STIs needed stabbing several times to traverse the entire range of gears. But the biggest advantage for Campagnolo was the fact that, unlike Shimano, they could be rebuilt – new springs and carrier ratchets could be replaced once worn. Where Shimano was a throwaway technology, for Campagnolo obsolescence was less of an issue.

Campagnolo's gear shift can be done from a variety of different hand positions and their levers can be placed on the handlebars in a wide range of positions while retaining easy access to the shift and still allowing reach for pulling on the brakes. Smaller hands preferred Campagnolo over Shimano, although neither was designed with women in mind.

However, just like Shimano, Campagnolo have redesigned the shape of their levers three times. The first shape was large, to accommodate the mechanism and allow long levers for mechanical advantage. As the shift on the smaller gear lever was pretty heavy going, the brakes had also been redesigned and the cable routing was more direct. The next shape was ergonomically simpler – the mechanism shrank slightly and the brake levers were now carbon (for the Record group). They had a more sculpted profile and felt easier on the fingers under sustained braking. Best of all, there was considerable weight saving. Like Shimano they added extra buttons for their computer system, the strangely named Ergobrain.

The latest incarnation incorporates an all-round far better feeling lever, with a longer, smoother action to the brake lever and a sweeter, crisper shift. The natural riding position is better and the braking feels lighter and more responsive than the previous versions. Paradoxically, they look very un-Campagnolo though – slightly over-designed perhaps?

Impressions and opinions of the new breed of Ergopower lever have been mixed. Campagnolo have stepped into the 11-speed domain, just as Shimano have stepped into electronic. Could this be a technology too far? Campagnolo's extra sprocket and complete incompatibility with any other wheelset or groupset could be the thing that actually works against them.

Claimed weight: 338g

Materials: Carbon gear and brake levers with titanium internal parts

Speeds: Ten rear and double front chainwheels (triple available)

Compatibility: All Campagnolo 11-speed groups only

Shimano Dura-Ace 7900

Shimano 'flippers' are different from SRAM and Campagnolo for one fundamental reason. The up-shift on Shimano's road controls is activated by the brake lever, while the down-shift is activated by a secondary lever, placed behind the brake lever. The main lever is larger than any of their rival's gear levers and it provides a huge mechanical advantage for shifting the gear mechanisms. A big gain with Shimano's approach was the multi-tasking that could be achieved. The ability to shift and brake at the same time – the lever simultaneously moves inwards and to the side – may seem a small thing, but it was a distinct advantage for certain applications.

The result is a marked improvement in the speed and effort of the shift. This long lever also means that there is less of a positive 'click' in the indexing of the gears. The smaller down-shift lever can get a little 'lost' behind the brake lever, and when wearing big winter gloves it can be a bit of a fiddle to operate, but it's still the smoothest gear control on the market, so good that it's sometimes hard to tell if you have actually changed gear.

Historically Dura-Ace has only ever worked with its component family, thus only allowing full groupset compatibility. The shifting often worked only with Dura-Ace derailleurs whose geometry was specifically designed for their pro-level group. This meant a considerable investment if you wanted full pro-level Shimano gears, which was a big issue for riders on a budget. What became a bigger issue, down the line, was that Shimano gears were less serviceable than Campagnolo gears, and once they were worn out, they were useless. This led to the coining of the phrase that 'while Campagnolo wore in, Shimano wore out'.

Six-speed indexed gears went to seven when STI first arrived on the scene, then Shimano added an eighth sprocket and, eventually, a ninth. In 2003 Shimano followed Campagnolo (for once) in the sprocket leapfrog and they brought STI into 10-speed. Shimano had allowed for more gears by redesigning their hubs as well as their shifters (see also Hubs, page 78), but the analysis remains that Shimano's dogged determination to make the entire bike Shimano equipped and a step closer to total compatibility comes at a cost to durability. The search for a slicker gear shift meant that materials were pushed to the limit, so although the entirety worked very well, the question became, for how long?

The latest lever has followed Campagnolo and SRAM by allowing for the cables to be secured under the bar tape. This isn't the only improvement, however, as Shimano have added a reach adjustment screw in the lever so smaller hands and shorter fingers can custom tune the reach of the lever and the new hood design on their Dura-Ace and Ultegra components allow for many more hand holds for different riding positions than previous incarnations. The overall result allows for a cleaner-looking clutter-free bike with no flapping cables and a better fit for any hand size. Overall Shimano have matched their rivals for style and function, improving on ergonomics and retaining their trademark effortless shift.

There is still an element of complication in Shimano's designs. The current lever has an inordinate amount of working parts. Does this mean that there's more to go wrong? Perhaps, but the parts have all been included for better function. After all, as they say themselves, Dura-Ace is the Pursuit of Perfection.

Claimed weight: 379g

Materials: Carbon brake lever with titanium fixing hardware

Speeds: Ten rear and double front chainwheels

Compatibility: Shimano 10-speed derailleurs, cassettes and chains

SRAM Red

SRAM is an interesting company. It is actually an amalgamation of several companies that have brought together some excellent brands and factories with a wealth of experience – and these have been around for a while. Be it in chain and sprocket manufacture or cable and wheel production, they have assembled a powerful company with plenty of the market share. The major force behind them was German company Sachs, who had one of the longest histories in cycling and who had made more sprockets and chains than most.

You can't mention SRAM without mentioning mountain biking. Their heritage lies in the single track and downhills of the Mountain Bike World Cup circuit, and off-road racing in particular has always been their speciality. And when it comes to gears and braking one thing is certain – this market requires excellent controls. Handling and safety are always an issue with off-road riding and this means their grip shift twist gear shifters, handlebar mounted gear shifters and brake levers are designed with control in mind.

It took SRAM a long time to enter the road-racing market but they have made some big gains over the two existing market leaders in a short space of time. In 2006 the first groups featured a lever that was ergonomically superior to those from both Shimano and Campagnolo. They spent a considerable amount of R&D time on the ergonomics because they had less to fit into the lever housing, and the result is compact and suitable for all types of hand positions and hand sizes.

Rather than complicate the mechanism even further SRAM have simplified the engineering inside the lever housing. Double tap is self-explanatory – one shift lever requires two types of movement to do the up-shift and the down-shift. An inward push on the gear lever facilitates the up-shift while a single tap in the same direction clicks the lever and shifts down the sprockets. They have achieved this with very few moving parts. This makes the brake lever independent of the shift lever, and the resulting lack of friction improves the braking and keeps the two operations independent of each other.

The single lever allows for several hand positions while shifting up and down the gears and, although the technique is alien to both Campagnolo and Shimano users, it is intuitive and accurate. Best of all, there are fewer compatibility issues with industry standard wheels and cassettes, as with Campagnolo. Double tap takes some getting used to, but nevertheless it is a real alternative to shifters from Italy and Japan. It is also considerably lighter in weight.

Weight: 280g

Materials: Carbon gear and brake lever titanium, aluminium mechanism

Speeds: Ten rear and double front chainwheels only

Compatibility: All SRAM road derailleurs and industry standard 10-speed cassettes and chains (so, Shimano 10, but not Campagnolo 10)

Traditional Controls

Certain situations and special one-off bikes need old skool approaches to solve the shifting and braking control. A lot of this stuff works really well and much of it receives the same material technology and design attention as the standard top-level road groupset. I like to think that it's a good thing, because not all road bikes are intended for the same application. The obvious bike application that a professional rider would need such things for is a time-trial bike, which can't use the same components designed for drop bars – the nature of the aero-tuck has meant that the bike and handlebar design require a specific approach.

DOWN TUBE SHIFTERS
Although most racers will want Ergopower, Double Tap or STI, many riders still want the simplicity and serviceability that is allowed from the individual brake lever and a down tube-mounted shift lever. The advantages are that there is a more 'immediate' feel to the gear shift, and fewer cable management problems means less friction – the result is sharper shifts. Down tube shifters are easier to fix, seem to last much longer and look traditional. On a commuter bike or a training hack they make a lot of sense – as on an everyday bike, 'easy to fix' can be a good thing.

FLAT BAR SHIFTERS
Flat bar road bikes need special shifters that usually work the same way as those on mountain bikes. These are usually separate from the brake lever, but Campagnolo have combined brake and shift levers. Flat bar controls add comfort to a more upright touring or commuting position and the fact that the high-end groupsets from all the main manufacturers have a flat bar control set-up shows that there is a considerable market for a comfortable gear and brake solution.

BAR END CONTROLS
Originally designed by Campagnolo and widely used by professional riders in the 1950s, 'bar-cons' became a permanent feature on cyclo-cross bikes and were used by generations of rough-stuff riders. These shift

Top to bottom Shimano Dura-Ace down tube shifters, SRAM trigger shifters (for flat bars), then one of a pair of Shimano bar-end shifters (which can, with adapters, be used as thumb shifters on flat bars).

levers are a very practical approach to keeping the gear controls close to hand, at the end of a drop bar. They have had a bit of a renaissance in the past ten years or so, mainly owing to the nature of time-trial bikes and the fact that the open end of an aero bar is a great place to put them. Riders often need to have the bars pre-cut as the controls add extra length to the handlebars and aero extensions. The cables are taped under the bar tape or can be threaded through the bar to maximize the aerodynamic advantage.

STANDARD AERO LEVERS

The first aero levers allowed riders to lose the flapping cable that attached the lever to the brake stirrup. They first appeared on the road scene in the late 1980s and quickly established a following with professional riders who wanted extra comfort when riding with their hands close to the brake lever. They have become particularly popular on fixed-gear and single-speed road bikes.

TIME TRIAL BRAKE LEVERS

The bar end brake lever is another old design revisited for the time-trial market. They also have cables concealed under tape or threaded through the handlebar and they are often minimally shaped, again to give maximum aero advantage.

Top to bottom SRAM bar-end shifters, primarily designed for time-trial bikes, a standard Campagnolo brake lever (i.e. no shifting capability – it just works the brakes) and a SRAM brake lever for time-trial handlebars.

Controls

Brakes

'Campagnolo, SRAM and Shimano all use variations on the theme of the dual pivot system, which now applies considerable force to the rim with very little input at the levers. The result is improved stopping power and a more subtle feel at the levers.'

For many years, road bikes had the worst possible type of braking systems. Relying on basic friction between the pads and the rim, the brakes had to cope with all sorts of weather conditions. The poor quality components meant that brakes were difficult and tiring to operate on long mountain descents, often 'fading' as the pads deteriorated. Braking was both strenuous and ineffective and caused all sorts of hand pain.

Frames had bigger clearances too, so brakes needed a longer drop. This added to the mechanical problems as all the extra leverage on the pivots allowed by these bigger brake arms meant that the brakes could shake loose. As frames became racier in design brakes had to adapt. Campagnolo recognized this with their piccolo brake stirrup, which was neater and simpler than before, with shorter arms that felt solid and flex-free. But the weak link in the system, the lever, was unaltered, the cable looping out from the top of the brake lever hood with little return assistance. This still created problems for riders as it seemed that most of the force was being applied to the rim with the fingers.

Levers were redesigned many times during the 1980s and 1990s when concealing the cables 'aero-style' was popularized. Suntour and Shimano added return springs to the lever to assist the feel, and in time the cables improved too (largely thanks to Shimano's SLR cable system with nylon internal sleeves to reduce friction), as brake stops added to the top tube rear brake cables required less of the outer casing that had previously added extra friction.

Various caliper designs have been tried; centre pull, cantilever, Shimano's Para-pull and Campagnolo's beautiful, yet flawed, Delta brake. Fortunately, braking has become fast and effective over the past few decades – tighter frame clearances allowing smaller and more efficient brake calipers. Campagnolo, SRAM and Shimano all use variations of the dual pivot system, which now applies considerable force to the rim with very little input at the levers. The result is improved stopping power and a more subtle feel at the levers.

Shimano and Campagnolo have always done a particularly good job of forging brake arms and the best road brakes are made from cold-forged aluminium. This means that the brake arms can be made minimal but still retain the material strength when cold-forged into the required shape. They are now very low in reach with a brake-pad height adjustment of 40–50mm ($1^1/_2$–2ins) (measured from brake fixing bolt to brake shoe nut).

CNC-machined calipers are becoming increasingly popular – they can be very light (around 190g/$6^1/_2$oz a pair), and they certainly look different from those made by Shimano, SRAM and Campagnolo. The biggest problem is that they do not seem to have the structural integrity of a forged brake arm and, in my experience, they tend to transfer a lot of the hard work into the pivots, which suffer if they are neglected and left poorly adjusted. These brakes need a lot of servicing and, worse than that, the adjustment of the cables and the setting of the preferred travel of the lever is often compromised.

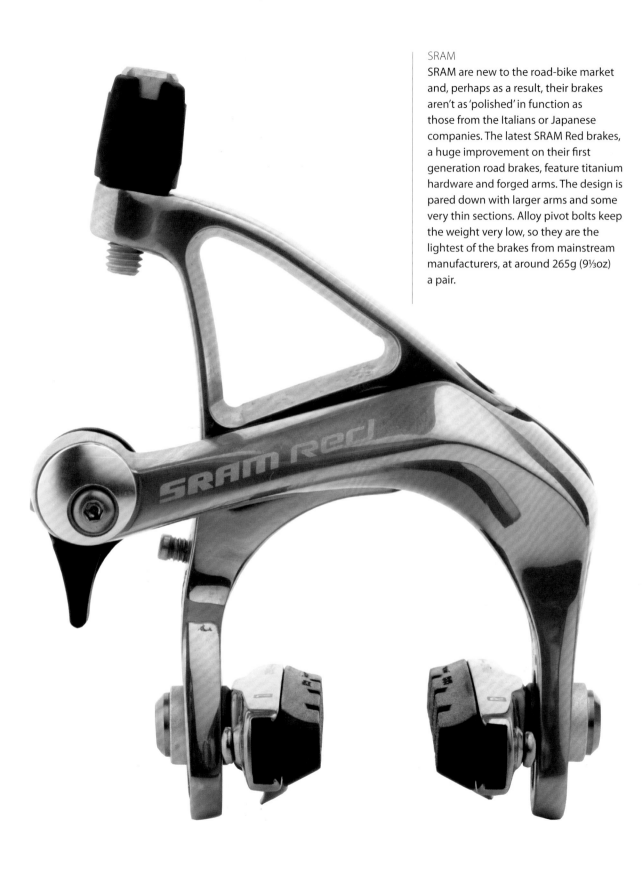

SRAM

SRAM are new to the road-bike market and, perhaps as a result, their brakes aren't as 'polished' in function as those from the Italians or Japanese companies. The latest SRAM Red brakes, a huge improvement on their first generation road brakes, feature titanium hardware and forged arms. The design is pared down with larger arms and some very thin sections. Alloy pivot bolts keep the weight very low, so they are the lightest of the brakes from mainstream manufacturers, at around 265g (9⅓oz) a pair.

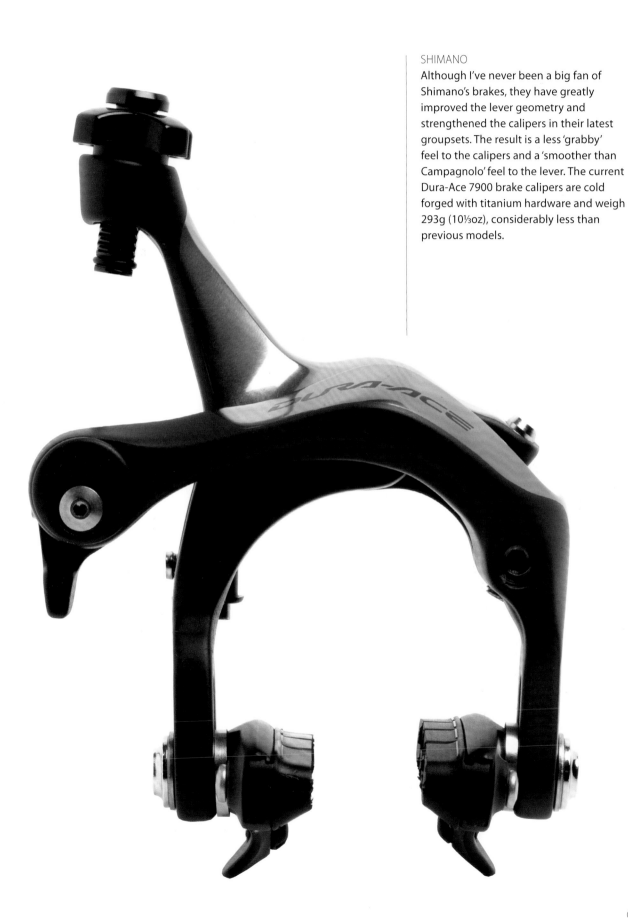

SHIMANO

Although I've never been a big fan of Shimano's brakes, they have greatly improved the lever geometry and strengthened the calipers in their latest groupsets. The result is a less 'grabby' feel to the calipers and a 'smoother than Campagnolo' feel to the lever. The current Dura-Ace 7900 brake calipers are cold forged with titanium hardware and weigh 293g (10⅓oz), considerably less than previous models.

CAMPAGNOLO

My preferred brake is the current Campagnolo Record, in either their cut-away 'skeleton' design (pictured here) or their previous 'solid' form. Both designs use the differential rear brake that is used in all their top-end groupsets. Campagnolo have realized that the front brake needs to be more powerful than the rear, as most of the braking is done on the front wheel. So they launched the 'double front fulcrum' front brake and a standard 'single pivot' on the rear. This differential approach is basically a simple old skool rear brake with a dual pivot design front.

This means that Campagnolo can save material in the rear brake and thus save some weight. The result is a consistent feel at the lever and less grabbing of the rim when braking under pressure or in an emergency. The current Super Record brakes claim a weight of 275g, which is only a little less than Shimano Dura-Ace 7900 and 10g more than SRAM's Red brakeset.

BRAKE PADS

Aluminium and carbon rims require different pad compounds. Always use the pad that the manufacturer recommends, as using an aluminium pad on a carbon rim can wear out the braking surface and damage the rim, while using softer carbon compound pads on aluminium rims can be inefficient and even dangerous. Mixing brake pads will provide unpredictable results, so if you use expensive wheelsets expect to pay close attention to your pad choice and serviceability.

Brake pads are held in a shoe, an aluminium-backed holder with a slot that allows the pad to be replaced easily. SRAM and Shimano use the same pattern shoe, which uses a retaining screw to secure the pad into the shoe and prevent it sliding out when the brake is applied. Campagnolo use a tight-fitting pad that is braced at the closed end of the shoe, which prevents it sliding out under braking forces. The Campagnolo and Shimano systems both use a different fixing bolt, so they can't be interchanged.

You will drag the brakes more in wet weather than in dry, making constant adjustments to the speed of the bike. In the dry braking can be applied later and for shorter periods of time. In my experience Shimano and SRAM compound brake pads are notoriously soft and have a very low profile from new, so they can wear out in a single wet ride, while Campagnolo's pads are much thicker in profile, perform better in the wet and wear out more slowly. However, both are predictable and steady wearing in the dry.

CABLE ROUTING

British bikes traditionally used the right-hand brake lever to activate the front brake (as on a motorbike) and the left-hand lever for the rear brake. Continental braking is the opposite. Neither is better, it's just a personal preference. However, riding a bike that is routed differently from what you are used to can be really dangerous, so don't be tempted to experiment before a trip to the Pyrenees. However you decide to route them, the cables need to be well-serviced to keep the system friction-free.

DEEP DROP BRAKES

Bikes with longer wheelbases, mudguards and larger tyre clearances need deeper drop brakes, simply so that they will fit around the tyre and wheel while still reaching the rim. The brake needs to be deeper than the usual racing brake – current models by Shimano allow for up to 57mm (2¼ins) of brake drop, while the standard road-racing brake is only up to 50mm (2ins).

Right Brake pads come in a variety of specialist flavours – after the standard pads there are special compounds for carbon rims, wet weather etc.

Cantilever Brakes

Cyclo-cross requires some special modifications to the standard road groupset. Apart from the gearing and the frame changes the main difference is the brakes. Cantilever brakes are supposedly more powerful than standard road brakes, although they don't really have the efficiency and modulation of the latest dual-pivot road brakes.

In the early days of cyclo-cross the brakes for those 'in the know' were Modolo and Mafac. Again, these Italian and French manufacturers made sets of totally non-adjustable, but completely 'right'-looking, cantilever brakes. Often confused with brakes with power they had one nut for pad retention and adjustment, so if you had wonky frame bosses you could expect squealing banshee brakes. However, although they were predictably awful, they did succeed in keeping the tyres free to spin in the frame without becoming bunged up with leaves and mud.

Cantilever brakes don't have the best action and need strong return springs to keep them moving freely. As a result they often feel a bit hard to pull, so easy brake set-up and maintenance is a consideration when building a cyclo-cross bike. The technology has hardly changed, even though materials and brake pads have improved the geometry of the brake, and the action is pretty crude. The latest breed of ergo levers has improved the feel at the lever, but they are still very difficult to get right.

Empella's Frog Legs have become the popular choice for professional cyclo-cross riders in Belgium and continental Europe (where cyclo-cross is a big winter sport). Pauls Components, TRP and Spooky all make good versions of the cantilever brake that has been stopping cross bikes for over 50 years.

Cable Systems

Brake Cables

Like tyres and chains, brake cables have origins that go back over 100 years. The basic design has remained almost the same since then. Attributed to several inventors, it was Raleigh Cycles in Nottingham that first developed the use of the cable for the bicycle. The Bowden cable (named after its inventor, Ernest Bowden) is a tightly coiled metal outer casing, coated in plastic or nylon, with an inner cable (or wire) that can move through the outer cable. This replaced rod brakes on bicycles and enabled bikes to have better brakes, controlled from the handlebars. Things remained more or less unchanged for over 60 years, with riders using cable-activated brakes and eventually derailleurs with down tube levers and a short section of Bowden cable at the rear derailleur.

In the late 1980s Shimano's SLR braking system brought a significant improvement to the brake cable outer casings, by adding a Teflon liner to the inside of the outer cable and a smoother braid to the inner wire. The results were impressive, and before very long all cables were made this way. Brake cables for modern road bikes are 1.6mm thick and have a stepped pear-shaped nipple at one end. The casings are now covered in a hard plastic.

Gear Cables

As gear components became more complicated and set-up more critical, gear cables had to be made to tighter tolerances. During the development of the SIS gear system Shimano improved the outer gear housing by making the metal element stranded rather than coiled, as the coiled cable compressed slightly under force, preventing accurate gear shifts. They also made their outer cables thinner, thereby adding flexibility. Although all gear cable outers are susceptible to damage when crashing and can split, they are a huge improvement on previous gear cables. All gear inner cables are 1.2mm in diameter, with a small barrel nipple at one end.

SHIMANO

Like most things Shimano do well, their cables are produced to exceptionally high standards. Dura-Ace cables have metal ferrules for the short section of gear cable to the derailleur and pre-fitted ferrules on the STI cable lengths.

SRAM

SRAM have used Gore RideOn cables systems. Their basic low-friction cable system is very good and certainly a match for Shimano and Campagnolo in quality. RideOn Bicycle Cable Systems were introduced in 1993 and quickly became very popular with mountain bikers. Ten years later they inexplicably stopped making them, although recently, realizing they still have a following, they relaunched them and added them to the SRAM road groupsets. Special cable treatments are added to the inner cables and the cable liners make great shifting and braking cables. They are very light too.

CAMPAGNOLO

Campagnolo Ergopower cables are sold in complete sets and the brake and gear cables follow the same pattern as Shimano with nylon inner sleeves and special Campagnolo grease pre-loaded into the end of the gear outers. The only real difference is they use plated brass end ferrules, which look a lot neater than the plastic ones supplied by Shimano. They run very smoothly, are very easy to install and are a lot cheaper than Shimano or SRAM cable sets. One major gripe is that they never supply enough ferrules to build a complete bike.

Opposite Standard gear cables.
Below Brake cables are thicker and have pear-shaped nipples.
Right Nokon's modular system.

NOKON

This German design is the only non-PVC covered cable system available. I really like this system on bikes with awkward cable routings, such as time-trial bikes, or bikes that have difficult-to-reach brake mounts, such as cyclo-cross bikes, or on smaller frames that can't have long, free-flowing cable sections.

Unlike a traditional 'Bowden' set-up, with different types of housings for brake and gear cables, Nokon cables feature one system for both, with different-sized ends for brake and gear stops. The cable housing is made from small aluminium ferrules laced together like beads in a popper necklace and threaded onto a glass fibre-reinforced Teflon liner. The clever bit is that each aluminium bead has a rounded top and a concave bottom, meaning that they will fit together and lock into each other, allowing for flexibility while remaining kink resistant. You can simply replace the liner and the inner wire when things start to seize up so they are easily recycled into new cable runs, without having to buy a completely new cable run. Perfect.

Nokon's standard aluminium system is 40 per cent lighter than a standard set of Bowden cables, corrosion free and compression resistant, so they feel more positive at the lever than standard brake cables and the gear shift is more 'instant' feeling. The only downside is the initial cost, but they do last well. Want to spend a fortune? Well, they make them in carbon too.

Independent Fabrication

Independent Fabrication
86 Joy St. (rear)
Somerville
MA 02143
USA
www.ifbikes.com
+1 617 666 3609

Independent Fabrication (IF) isn't just one builder, which is why they fill that gap between the big name company and the small one-man builders. Formed in 1995, they were born out of Fat City Cycles, one of the most innovative mountain bike companies of the early 1990s. When Fat closed its factory in Somerville, Massachusetts, it left behind a handful of workers: fabricator Lloyd Graves, welder Mike Flanigan and machinist and toolmaker Jeffrey Buchholz. They joined forces with Sue Kirby, Ben Cole and Steve Elmes to start building a bigger range of bikes alongside the best steel mountain bike frames the industry had ever seen. The Deluxe and the Special mountain bike frames were hugely popular.

Their benchmark road bikes, which followed soon after – The Crown Jewel (a road bike) and the Planet Cross (a 'cross-inspired frame) – are renowned as competent and were well received by the cycling press. In 1999, Tom Burnett and Tyler Evans joined IF from Merlin Metalworks, bringing titanium welding and fabrication experience from the then market leaders. In 2000 they produced their first titanium bikes, and latterly the XS, their current flagship bike. With this bike Independent Fabrication showed a unique take on road-bike building, using carbon mainframe tubes and welded titanium lugs. They made an amazing bike that has won several awards and accolades from the cycling press and industry.

IF bikes aren't the lightest or the most race-proven bikes out there, but the things that make them good, are very good. They ride exceptionally well, they look amazing and close attention has been paid to the details. IF adapt quickly, producing variants of standard bikes with single speed or fixed versions – fun bikes they certainly are. Throughout their range the machining and finishing is spot on and the 'Independent' nature of the design and graphics makes them a lot less corporate looking, which is what is so refreshing about IF. The best way I can describe them is that they don't take themselves too seriously and yet care deeply about what they do.

'It's a passionate group of people. We're lucky enough to have the chance to make money out of our hobby.'

This interview is with the company's design, finance and sales director, Joe Ingram.

Materials used:
We use steel, titanium, Reynolds 953 and carbon fibre. Every frame is fully custom and we have many wall thicknesses and tube diameters in all materials so we can dial in ride quality based on a rider's height, weight and riding style.

Employees:
11: Lloyd, Jamie, Tyler, Gary, Bee, Leah, Clint, Finn, Kevin, Shawn and Joe.

Price range:
US$1,900–6,000 for the frame and fork. This is custom inclusive but the price can go up if there is fancy paint.

Waiting period (average!):
Turnaround time from the sign-off of the frame design is currently seven weeks.

Frames built per year:
Last year we built around 1,000 frames.

Who are your customers and how would you 'define' them?
Our customers come from all walks of life. We have the wealthy cycling enthusiast and the young racer or bike shop employee.

How long have you been building bikes?
Since 1995.

Do you make (or have you made) frames for any professional riders or teams?
We have made frames for Tim Johnson, Harlan Price, Sarah Uhl and Gianna Roberge (world champion). We currently have a men's road team and a grassroots race team. Harlan Price was the first American to get top 10 at La Ruta in 2008.

What started your interest in bicycle engineering/design?
I started working at bike shops in college and fell in love with the sport. When I began working at IF I relished the opportunity to learn more about frame design and construction. I learned everything I know about frame design from several people here at IF. Lloyd, Tyler and Jamie have a wealth of knowledge that is simply incredible. Their passion for the sport and understanding of materials and frame design pushed me to learn as much as I could.

Who influences what you do now (if not all of the above)?
Honestly, we are influenced by our customers, as every design is so different. Even those designs with similar geometry will have different tubes selected. Communication is key and the more I find out about the customers the better equipped I am to design them the perfect bicycle.

What is the best material for frame manufacturing (and why)?
It depends on who you ask and what you are looking to get out of the bicycle. We are pretty agnostic when it comes to materials. Some materials excel in areas like strength or stiffness but that doesn't necessarily make them better. Some materials require extra care when building because you run the risk of contamination but we have the right tools to ensure that every frame is dialled in to each customer's needs and wants.

How do you size your customers?

We work almost exclusively through IF dealers. A customer would go into a shop to get fitted and then that information would be sent to IF. We can work with any fit system out there. Obviously the raw body dimensions and position numbers are important but we also want to know as much as possible about riding style, health issues and rider goals and objectives.

What is the most exciting new development in frame design or tubing technology?

We are really excited about our new full carbon bike (Oracle). It uses new, proprietary tooling that enables us to generate fully custom, bladder-moulded lugs out of the highest quality carbon available. Other things that get me excited are sometimes not all that new but just continue to amaze. The Factory Lightweight is one of the lightest bikes we make and the ride quality you get from a beautifully welded steel frame is simply amazing.

The Custom Road Bike

What's the most important element to the frame?

The fit. Everyone is different in size and riding style. The marriage of the frame with the components should put riders in a position to get the most out of the sport and to meet and exceed their individual goals.

What do you want to achieve for your customers?

Enjoyment on the bicycle. We want you to love the bike that we create for you. It should fit perfectly and generate a ride quality that constantly gets you excited about riding. This excitement will lead to the fulfilment of other goals. The more fun you have on the bike the more you want to ride and this will lead to increased speed, weight loss or any other objectives you may set for yourself. I like to think that we make some of the nicest TIG welded and custom carbon frames available today. The materials we use, the attention to detail and quality of product help us to produce a beautifully tailored bicycle for each customer.

Who is/was the best frame manufacturer or builder and why?

There are so many fantastic builders out there. Everyone excels in something different. If you are looking for a gorgeous lugged frame then Bruce Gordon or Richard Sachs are sure to fit the bill. I also have a tremendous amount of respect for Dario Pegoretti.

Independent Fabrication

The Gears

Bottom Brackets

For much of the road-racing bicycle's history standard road frames have had threads that accept the bottom bracket unit. Until there is a huge change in design and approach, this is the way that manufacturers expect the design to continue (see also Frame Design, page 38).

Initially the bottom bracket was made up of several working parts: the axle; the bearings; and the frame cups that acted as bearing races, kept the whole thing tight and allowed it to be adjusted and maintained. For many years this was fine, as long as the unit was maintained and kept well adjusted, but there were limitations, especially when manufacturers added more gears, making chainlines and crank alignment an increasingly important issue. Shimano, busily reinventing the bicycle drivetrain, devised a bottom bracket system that made the whole unit a single piece, introducing the age of the throwaway bearing unit and the demise of the adjustable system. Campagnolo followed suit soon afterwards and they both made units that were easy to install and specifically machined to fit their own range of cranks.

Square Taper

There were two types of square taper crank, JIS (Japanese Industry Standard), which was used by Shimano, and ISO (International Organization for Standardization), which is the taper Campagnolo used. Although Campagnolo and Shimano have moved on, there are still many smaller manufacturers making excellent square taper bottom brackets. Royce, Phil Wood and White Industries all make excellent brackets in a variety of sizes and standards, so if you are happy with square taper, there is no reason to throw it all away.

Royce titanium square taper bottom bracket.

Octalink

Shimano redesigned their cranks and produced the Octalink, a tubular bottom bracket axle with a splined end, and applied it to their mountain bike and road bike groupsets. Octalink was intended to reduce the issues with over-tightened square taper cranks, lighten up the bottom bracket and add some more stiffness

'Octalink wasn't a huge improvement and it certainly had its problems, but the days of the square taper bottom bracket were nearly over.'

to the pedalling process. Octalink wasn't a huge improvement and it certainly had its problems, but the days of the square taper bottom bracket were nearly over. Other smaller independent manufacturers looked at the Octalink system and came up with the ISIS (International Splined Interface Standard) drive, which was adopted mainly in the mountain bike arena.

BB30

Cannondale introduced this variation on the threaded bottom bracket design for both road and mountain bikes. Although the idea is a good one and even though Cannondale made this technology available to all builders, it's going to take time to catch on in the conservative frame building and design world. The main issue is that modern frames all have the same threads, so any bracket can be found to fit almost any frame, no matter who made it or when it was made. This makes the frame versatile and allows riders to select whatever component system they want, but it does create issues with wide bottom brackets (especially for triple chainsets) and it's not the best solution. BB30 removes the threaded cups from the frame and replaces them with press-fit bearing units, thus making it possible to reduce the width of the bracket and to fit a variety of chainset configurations.

SHIMANO INTEGRATED BOTTOM BRACKETS

Shimano totally redesigned the bottom bracket and the crank fixings with an external bearing or integrated bottom bracket. Launched with the Dura-Ace groupset in 2004, this was a big step forward from attaching the cranks to a bottom bracket axle. With integrated cranks the bearings threaded into the frame and sat outside the bottom bracket shell. The crank had the axle attached to it and it is simply pushed through the

Above SRAM crankset to fit the BB30 standard introduced by Cannondale.

holes in the bearing units and clamped into place with the left-hand crank. The result is very stiff and incredibly simple.

SRAM INTEGRATED BOTTOM BRACKETS

Truvativ (SRAM's crank company) followed suit and made several cranks with external bottom bracket units. SRAM have a choice of ceramic Black Box bearings in their top end Red groupset. Italian component makers FSA also produce a variety of integrated cranks and bottom brackets.

CAMPAGNOLO ULTRA TORQUE

Campagnolo's take on the external bearing bottom bracket and crank system, Ultra Torque, came to light in 2006. The cups are based on the same principle as Shimano's system but the bearings are attached to the ends of the axle on the inside of each crank arm. It is slightly more complicated to fit than Shimano but is very neatly finished, with no clamps or allen bolts and the cranks are narrower. The bearings can be replaced.

CHRIS KING

If you are considering aftermarket bottom bracket cups for your Shimano cranks, this is the answer for perfect bearings. The best thing about the Chris King unit is that you can easily service the bearing and replace the grease with a simple grease gun, purging the old grease and replacing it with new grease. This is something that Shimano would never do (they prefer the obsolescence of a throwaway unit). Chris King brackets fit Shimano external bearing Hollowtech II type cranks and some SRAM and FSA cranks. They also come in lots of different colours.

From the top SRAM, Campagnolo and Chris King external bottom bracket bearing units.

Cranks

There are many misconceptions about what makes a good pair of cranks, the arms of the unit that we refer to as the chainset. Chainsets are now used with external bearing bottom brackets, which place the bearings further apart than brackets that were fitted inside the frame. They therefore add some extra rigidity to the drive, but this brings its own set of design issues and problems.

For many years the system for chainsets was a square tapered bottom bracket axle – JIS for Shimano users and ISO for Campagnolo users. The taper on the bottom bracket axle was very slightly different, so cranks and brackets could not be interchanged. This meant that you had either a Campagnolo or a Shimano crank and couldn't mix and match.

Shimano decided to redesign the entire drivetrain and the result was a new type of bottom bracket that fitted on the outside of the bottom bracket shell. This sensibly used the standard road frame's bracket dimensions but placed the bearing to the outside of the bracket. It was a brave move but started the ball rolling on changing the whole system.

I am not convinced that the current Campagnolo Ultra Torque and Shimano Hollowtech II systems are much of an improvement in function and serviceability over the square taper bottom-bracketed cranks of a decade or so ago. The external bearing cranks were intended to increase stiffness and they certainly seem to have provided a firmer feel to the pedals. However, they have a wider Q factor than previous double chainsets, aren't much lighter than previous generations of the Record or Dura-Ace road groups, and the bearings in the bottom bracket cups don't have the same interchangeability or longevity of a good-quality standard square taper bottom bracket unit.

Shimano Hollowtech II

Shimano have stuck with a drop forged aluminium hollow crank, a technology that they perfected and one that produces a considerably lighter crank. They tried carbon fibre but recognized its limitations and decided that aluminium was a far better process for them and remained affordable. The current Dura-

Ace 7900 unit is 725g (23½oz), including the bottom bracket cups, which is lighter than previous Dura-Ace cranks but by no means the lightest chainset you can buy. However, the function and form of the Dura-Ace crank are excellent, and the improvements easily outweigh the disadvantage of the extra grams.

Campagnolo Ultra Torque

Campagnolo followed Shimano into the external bottom bracket market in 2006. They had successfully added carbon fibre to the cranks on their chainsets in their last range of square taper cranks, but with mixed results. They were super lightweight, at around 500g (16oz) for the Record version, and they worked well enough, but many riders still preferred to use the aluminium crank from the previous groupset, claiming that it was stiffer and more reliable. Ultra Torque changed the

bottom bracket design and added more structural integrity to the chainset. The crank arms were made larger and the oversized axle was split into two halves bonded into either crank arm. This was joined in the centre of the axle with a splined Hirth joint and a 10mm (½in) allen nut. Campagnolo claim that this is easier to use and has better ergonomics than similar integrated set-ups. All this technology has made a very lightweight unit that tips the scales at just under 700g (23oz).

The Custom Road Bike

SRAM

Other external bottom bracket cranks are a fusion of the ideas that came from Shimano and Campagnolo. They usually have a captive bolt on the left-hand crank that secures the unit on the non-drive side. SRAM's main advantage is that it is really easy to install and requires only one allen key for installation and removal. SRAM's Red chainset has a carbon fibre spider and, at 750g (24oz), is heavier than Campagnolo and Shimano.

Compact or standard?

Compact drive cranks are lighter in weight than a triple set-up and are far more mountain friendly than a standard road chainset. They are currently very popular with anyone who doesn't want to race as they give a set of lower gears. For example, if you use regular 12–25-tooth cassette sprockets, a double 'standard' with 53/39 rings has a relatively high, 42.1–119.3ins range of gears for riding at higher speeds; a compact double chainset with 50/34 rings will offer gears that range from 35.7–109.5ins; and triple chainsets with 52/42/30 rings have a huge range of gears, from 31.5–113.9ins. So why use compact? They are lighter than triple chainsets, with less changing involved, and they have lower gears than a standard chainset, which places less strain on the drivetrain, but they can still be comfortably used for racing on the flat and touring around the Alps.

Bolt Circle Diameter (BCD)

This is sometimes referred to as PCD (Pitch Circle Diameter). Standard chainrings come in different BCD patterns. Shimano and Campagnolo standard road ring sizes are different and they have also decided to make their chainwheels even more shaped and profiled so that aftermarket rings struggle to fit their cranks. However, the latest compact cranks have stuck with an industry standard 110mm (4⅓in) BCD, so choice is much wider. Fortunately, track cranks all have the same BCD, which makes it easier to find aftermarket chainrings.

Track: 144mm (5⅝ins)
Smallest chainwheel 44-tooth

Shimano Standard road rings: 130mm (5¹⁄₁₀ins)
Smallest chainwheel 38-tooth

Campagnolo Standard road rings: 135mm (5⅓ins)
Smallest chainwheel 39-tooth

Compact: 110mm (4⅓ins)
All manufacturers, smallest chainwheel 34-tooth

CRANK ARMS AND LENGTH

It's always a bit tricky to advise exactly what is the right crank length. 170mm is the standard length for road cranks and is probably the standard that most people will start with. It's not always the case, but tall riders of 182cm (6ft) plus will usually opt for longer cranks – 175mm or 180mm – and riders under 167cm (5ft 6ins) will use shorter ones – 170mm or 165mm.

Custom-fitted bikes will take into account leg length and foot position over the pedals and this may mean that you will need the advice of an experienced fit technician.

Crank length

Bolt Circle Diameter

White Industries

I think that this VBC (Variable Bolt Circle) design crank from American bike component makers White Industries is a huge step up from previous crank systems. Its ingenious bolt system allows for a far greater variation in chainring sizes, so you can have standard or compact rings on the same crankset. The outer ring attaches directly to the crank arm; machined into this outer ring are five slots, designed to replace the traditional chainring bolt circle spider. The slots allow the inner ring to self-centre without being confined to a specific bolt circle. It's brilliant and saves all that fiddle time when swapping gear ratios for a trip to the mountains. You can vary the gears from a standard 52/38, down through compact sizes of 50/36, to as low as 38/24.

White Industries
VBC Road cranks

Chainline

Chains work best when they are travelling in a straight line from the chainwheels to the sprockets. This is why single-geared track drivetrains with a fixed wheel express the most effort into forward drive (this is one of the reasons why derailleurs took so long to catch on with the pro riders in the 1940s and 1950s). If you are to get the chainline as perfect as possible you need to pay close attention to the position of the chain on the chainwheels in relation to the cassette sprockets. Double cranks must be used with the correct bottom bracket to ensure that this chainline is spot on – anything peculiar in the set-up can alter the chainline dramatically and make the front gear shift awkward and unpredictable.

Q FACTOR

This is the distance between the two pedal faces of the cranks. Why is it important? Well, pedalling with your feet further apart can cause problems related to joint injury and pedalling efficiency. Taller riders will be less affected than shorter riders, who will have more bow in their legs with the same Q factor.

Track cranks with a single chainwheel can have a much narrower bottom bracket, and this usually means a low Q factor of around 130mm (5¹⁄₁₀ins). Some track riders have reduced this even further to maximize low-profile pedalling.

The problem with modern external bearing bottom brackets is that the extra width for the bottom bracket adds problems when keeping the Q factor low. Earlier square taper cranks, such as Dura-Ace 7400 and Campagnolo's Record, pre-Ultra Torque, had much lower Q factors – around 10mm (½in) less than the current external bearing cranks.

The average Q factor for a standard double crank with external bottom bracket seems to be 145mm (5¾ins), but it's much less than the 160mm (6⅓ins) on most triple chainrings and mountain bikes. This is the main reason why road riders opt for compact cranks for sportive bikes, as they can have a wide range of lower gear ratios without the extra Q factor.

Shoe cleat angle and shoe size will also have a bearing. People with very big feet can sometimes rub on the chainstay of the bike and this can mean that some frame designs, for example those with fatter chainstays (especially at the point where they meet the seatstays), prevent a narrow Q factor, so it's not always as simple as fitting a narrower crank arm to achieve a lower Q factor.

I'm not a big fan of triple cranks, because the wider Q factor can place your feet too far apart. I haven't heard of any problems using either Shimano's or Campagnolo's current standard double cranks, even though they have a wider Q factor than previous double chainsets. It is important to have your cleats set up properly first. Think about the alignment of your pedals and cleats first, before you start worrying about Q factor, which is important, but not as important as the contact point with the pedals.

Track cranks

Track racing bikes require a completely different set of cranks from that of a road bike and, although they are simple, single chainwheels on cranks create their own set of problems. Tracks are usually steeply banked, which means that at slower speeds the pedals are closer to the track surface. For this reason the bike is usually designed with a higher bottom bracket and the cranks are shorter to allow greater pedal clearance. However, shorter cranks are also used to aid acceleration, as they can be wound up to speed quickly.

Track cranks have a completely different spider from double cranks and align the chainline perfectly, which is why it is important to use the correct bottom bracket and crank. Interestingly, Campagnolo still make their track crank with a square taper bottom bracket and Shimano use an Octalink bracket, so they have both stuck with simple technology for the simplest drive system. Only SRAM make an external bearing track crank. All readily available track cranks are aluminium and forged. There are plenty of other options on the market for track bikes, most notably Sugino, Miche and Pauls Components.

TRACK GEARING

Track gearing is a science in itself. Gears on bicycles are expressed in inches, denoting the distance that the bike moves forward during one revolution of the pedal, whereas sprocket and chainring sizes are measured in the number of teeth. Most track racing bikes ready for the velodrome come with something in the region of 90ins (50-tooth chainwheel and a 15-tooth sprocket), although riders may change to a lower gear of 86ins (48 x 15) on outdoor tracks, on concrete, where rougher surfaces and windy conditions can slow things down a bit. Pursuit riders may go bigger, even up to 114ins (52 x 12) if they can sustain speeds of 55kmh (34mph) plus. All seasoned track racers have plenty of chainwheels and spare sprockets in their kitbags at each track event and may change up or down depending on the event and the conditions.

Left The simplicity and strength of a track crank, in the case from Truvativ. **Opposite** One of *the* finest examples, Campagnolo's exquisite Record offering.

Rear Derailleurs

Derailleurs are diverse in design and have been developed over 100 years of manufacture and innovation. The rear derailleur is the focal point of the modern racing bicycle. This ingenious mechanism was developed by several companies that were involved in the development of what we have today. In 1928 the first lever-operated gear change system was introduced. The Osgear, or Super Champion Gear, was a very involved system. Derailleurs were slow to come to the racing bike for a number of reasons, not all of which were sensible.

Derailleurs were banned from the Tour de France until 1937 and riders were still using fixed-wheel racing bikes that required swapping the wheel around. This wasn't ideal, especially in the mountains. Campagnolo's quest was to perfect the gear change and he devised a crude but effective system, the Cambio Corsa, which was used for over a decade.

The idea of using two or three sprockets at the rear wheel and a mechanism that derailed them soon followed, first operated with two cables (one to pull it in each direction) and then with a spring to assist the return. During the following decades several key cycling manufacturers (other than Shimano and Campagnolo) made derailleurs, most notably Galli, Ofmega and Gipiemme in Italy, and Mavic, Huret and Simplex in France. In Japan Suntour and Shimano made improvements to existing European designs and began to expand the possibilities.

The principle is pretty much the same across all the systems. Campagnolo now offer up to 11 sprockets at the rear wheel and this requires a very narrow chain. Shimano has the Dura-Ace electronic shifting system, similar to a car gear box. It is quicker and more accurate than before, but still relies on very tight tolerances in both the frame alignment and set-up of the complete system.

Interestingly, derailleurs became heavier when indexing began, and for several years there was a battle to get the function and shift accurate while saving weight, so pre-index derailleurs were considerably simpler and lighter than they are now. Some of them could cope with the throw of only seven sprockets, so the cassettes and chains were also redesigned.

Modern rear derailleurs are fairly complex but the operation and function remains relatively simple. They are cable activated and are controlled by the rider, at the handlebars, via a shifting lever that is now integrated into the brake lever. While it may once have been true that Campagnolo wore in and Shimano wore out, nowadays all gears wear out at the same rate and all feel pretty slick from day one.

'Campagnolo's quest was to perfect the gear change and he devised a crude but effective system, the Cambio Corsa, which was used for over a decade.'

Campagnolo Record

Campagnolo rear derailleurs always have an elegance that their competitors struggle to match. Generations of rear derailleurs from Campagnolo have been some of the most beautiful bicycle components ever made, especially the Record and Nuovo Record derailleurs of the 1970s and the C Record rear derailleur of the following decade. Campagnolo's current crop of 11-speed derailleurs is a nod to the past. The Super Record derailleur featured titanium bolts and forged aluminium body parts. In action Campagnolo have always been fast and responsive as well as beautiful. The 10-speed Record rear derailleur was good, and some say that the 11-speed is even better. Campagnolo still lead the way in beautifully designed and engineered components.

Shimano

Shimano perfected the index-geared groupset and made the first combined brake and gear lever. Their original quest for a fully integrated bike produced the SIS gear system, and now all the manufacturers make sure you are fully integrated, from derailleurs to chain. Shimano's derailleurs have always been made to exact tolerances and work impeccably. They lack the charm that Campagnolo always seems to achieve, but, until recently, their function was unmatched in precision and control.

SRAM

SRAM's derailleur design is based around the double tap control system that they introduced in 2006. As they come to the road bike market from the mountain bike market, it's no surprise that they take a completely different approach from that of Shimano or Campagnolo.

The Red rear derailleur comes with ceramic bearings, titanium springs and magnesium body parts. SRAM's shift takes some time to get used to if you have been using Shimano or Campagnolo, but it's impressively fast and precise and once set up needs little attention or fettling.

Lightweight RD

Carbon Sports (makers of Lightweight wheels) produce this all-carbon fibre rear derailleur that really has to be seen (and held) to be believed. Campagnolo certainly took some design cues from it when designing their 11-speed rear derailleur, but they just couldn't get close to the weight of the Lightweight RD. In rear derailleur stakes this 30–50g saving is considerable. Longevity is added to this expensive component with titanium parts, steel springs and ceramic bearings, which are used in the aluminium jockey (pulley) wheels. Carbon Sports don't just make expensive fancy carbon parts and widgets, though their product works and works well, and in this case it works with both Shimano and Campagnolo, although not SRAM shifters and cassettes.

Weights (manufacturers stated figures)

Lightweight (Campagnolo or Shimano): 120g

Campagnolo Record 10-speed: 184g

Campagnolo Super Record 11-speed: 172g

Shimano Dura-Ace 7900: 166g

Shimano Dura-Ace Di2: 222g

SRAM Red: 150g

Front Derailleurs

Although there are two types of fitting for front derailleurs, most front derailleurs have always fitted to the seat tube just above the chainset with a clamp. This clamp is integral to the derailleur; for frames with brazed-on brackets for front derailleurs (usually steel frames) there is an alternative clampless design.

Campagnolo Record
Previously standard double front derailleurs wouldn't work with compact drive chainsets, so a different gear component would have to be used to cope with the smaller chainrings on a compact. This creates obvious difficulties, so Campagnolo have redesigned the front derailleur to work with both compact and double chainrings. The problem now is that they don't work with old style shifters and 10-speed systems, so if you want 11-speed you will have to rebuild the entire gear system, which gets expensive. On the plus side, Campagnolo's 11-speed front shift is the quickest and easiest of all the groups and the carbon fibre cage plates look sleek and stylish. It weighs 71g (2½oz).

Shimano
Shimano's front derailleur was the first to be 'indexed', so rather than readjusting the gear lever constantly as the chainline shifted with rear derailleur movement, they made sure that the cage plates of the front derailleur stayed clear of the chain, touching it only when the gear lever was activated. When set up well it worked superbly, but poor cable tension and badly aligned derailleurs often made for annoying chain grating and rubbing. Shimano spent a lot of R&D time on the design of the shape of the cage plates in the latest Dura-Ace group. The current narrower 10-speed chain and ingenious cage redesign has made it 'trim-less'. Set up carefully it works well and, at 66g (2⅓oz), it's the lightest there is.

SRAM
SRAM's front derailleur works with compact and standard cranks, but the clever bit about their Red front derailleur is that it can be 'feathered' according to rear gear selection by using the front left-hand gear lever to micro adjust the position of the derailleur, thus allowing old skool adjustment – a very welcome addition for racing when gear selection can mean awkward chainlines and rubbing front mechs. Titanium cage plates on the Red derailleur add a certain sheen and keep the weight down to 71g (2½oz) for their braze-on only version.

PARLEE CARBON CLAMP
If you have a carbon tubed frame the chances are that it will not have a brazed-on front derailleur boss. Titanium frames rarely have a boss either, so using a clamp is essential. Parlee have made a really neat front derailleur band that weighs almost nothing. It's available in three sizes – 28.6mm (1¹⁄₁₀ins), 31.8mm (1¼ins) and 34.9mm (1⅓ins) – and fits all well-known front derailleurs for braze-on fittings.

The Custom Road Bike

Right Carbon-caged Campagnolo
Super Record front mech.

Opposite SRAM's Red front derailleur.
Right Shimano's Dura-Ace mech.

The Gears

Ernesto Colnago

Viale Brianza 9
20040 Cambiago
Milan
Italy
www.colnago.com
+39 02 95 30 80 82

'Ogni epoca ha un campione, ogni campione ha una Colnago'

'Every time has a champion, every champion has a Colnago'

Many new frame builders arrive on the scene with exciting new materials and manufacturing processes, but after over 50 years Ernesto Colnago still stands out as having the ability to innovate. But the real endorsement of the Colnago brand comes from bike racers, and that is where his story begun.

During the 1951 road racing season, Ernesto Colnago was riding in the amateur classic Milano–Busseto. During a tight final sprint, there was a massive crash and Colnago hit the deck. He broke his right leg and had to spend 50 days off the bike and off work. He asked his employer, Mr Focesi of Italian racing bike manufacturer Gloria Cycles, to send him wheels to build at home. Ernesto quickly realized he could make more money working at home. And Colnago's apprenticeship as a welder at Gloria meant he could build frames too. Three years later, in 1954, he opened his first, small workshop on via Cavour in Cambiago, near Milan. These early Colnagos were highly regarded by the local racing fraternity and, soon, many top stars called on his services – even those with other bike sponsors. He always worked hard and often stayed up all night, once building more than ten pairs of wheels for a local team the night before a big stage race. And in 1957, Gastone Nencini won the Giro d'Italia on one of his bikes.

His first innovative ideas were when he decided to create the first cold-forged bicycle forks in the early 1950s. After that, there was the lightest bicycle in the world (5.6kg), for Eddy Merckx to break the World Hour record in Mexico City on 25 October 1972. From this project, the Colnago 'Mexico' was born with it's innovative helical-shaped tubing.

The next important step for Colnago was in 1983 when the Cambiago workshop created two groundbreaking designs: the aerodynamic 'Oval CX' and what was to be the legendary road frame, the 'Master', with its revolutionary bi-conic star shape steel tubing. Colnago also created the first frameset in carbon fibre in collaboration with Ferrari Engineering in 1986. In 1989, the dramatic Colnago 'C35' emerged, an innovative monocoque carbon fibre frame in road racing and mountain bike versions. And not long after along came the 'Carbitubo', a carbon fibre frame with two parallel down tubes, and in 1991 the 'Bititan', a lighter frame made from titanium.

But it was his Master which came to be the Colnago design that everyone wanted. Colnago developed a cast bottom bracket shell with an integrated web that avoided the necessity for a chainstay bridge and added an improved seat stay design and compact brake bridges. As a result Colnago Masters were stiffer and more responsive than previous steel frames, but above all the supple, safe and reassuring ride was retained, which is what continues to be a part of every Colnago frame today. They were never the lightest of bikes, but rode predictably and were blessed with the ability to take considerable punishment, whatever material they were made from.

It wasn't just the frame that Colnago improved on the Master and subsequent frame designs. As bike technician and Colnago enthusiast Rohan Dubash recalled in a feature in *Rouleur* magazine, 'The Master was a huge leap for racing bicycle design, but it also saw the introduction of the now-ubiquitous Colnago Precisa straight fork. This design confounded the critics at the time and is still widely misunderstood today. Colnago knew that in long arduous races, the fresher rider who had wasted the least energy would be best positioned to win. Stiffness ensured efficiency — but at the expense of comfort and vibration absorbency. This ultimately contributed to rider fatigue. Engineers at Ferrari showed how, in reality, a straight fork actually reduced the transmission of road shock to the rider. The advent of the microfusion fork crown then gave Colnago the strength to create the rake at the top of the fork, as opposed to along its length. The added benefits of a blade under less stress and with no compromise to wall thickness gave us the unmistakable straight fork that now graces every Colnago.'

1994 was a halcyon year for Colnago as they introduced the 'C40' carbon fibre frameset for the company's 40th anniversary. This is still a benchmark racing frame today. No other frame has won as many races as the Colnago C40: from Paris–Roubaix to several World Championships. After ten years of success for the C40, Ernesto Colnago launched the C50 in 2004. It was his company's 50th anniversary.

In addition to Colnago having provided racing with some of its finest machines, his riding experience has also enabled him to spot several great riders before their potential was realized elsewhere: Giuseppe Saronni, Pavel Tonkov and Yaroslav Popovych have all been mentored by Ernesto. During the 1970s and 1980s, he would send 30 bikes a year to the former Soviet Union.

Today, he still helps young local racers who can't afford a bike, often giving them a second-hand one for races. He knows how hard the sport is and how important good equipment can be. He is acquainted with many of the riders personally and remembers every one of their victories, as any true fan of the sport would. Colnago's cycling sponsorship deals cost him around 530 bikes a year, all custom-made and approved by the man himself, which means cyclists who ride for a Colnago-backed team will certainly get what they want.

Fiorenzo Magni, Gastone Nencini, Eddy Merckx, Giuseppe Saronni, Gianni Motta, Gibì Baronchelli, Michele Dancelli, Gianni Bugno, Oscar Freire, Johan Museeuw, Tony Rominger, Pavel Tonkov, Yaroslav Popovych, Erik Zabel and Alessandro Petacchi. All these cycling stars share two things in common: between them they have won most of the big races on the professional racing

calendar and all of them did it aboard a bike designed and made by Ernesto Colnago. To date Colnago has assisted and supported 100 professional teams, with around 2,500 professional racers, who have clocked up more than 7,500 wins worldwide.

So the man who championed many of the racing bicycle frame's best advances was, like his compatriot Tullio Campagnolo two decades before him, a racer first and an engineer second.

Materials used:
Carbon, steel and aluminium.

Employees:
50

Price range:
From €1,500 to 10,000.

Waiting period (average!):
8 to 10 weeks, depending on the model requested.

Frames built per year (average):
Approximately 20,000 per year.

Who are your customers and how would you 'define' them?
Demanding, expert, experienced and cognizant.

How long have you been building bikes?
For 55 years.

Do you make (or have you made) frames for any professional riders or teams?
Yes always and for more than 200 teams over the years. The relationship between
the bike manufacturer and the sponsor is very important, it's like a family.
You need this relationship for the best results. For example, we worked with
Rabobank for ten years. And this association was a good example: Rabobank put
in the money, Colnago supplied the bicycles, and the riders put in the heart.
You need to work together.

What started your interest in bicycle engineering/design?
It was born with me.

Who taught you to build?
I started when I was thirteen years old to work for the Gloria factory in Milan.
It was 25 November 1946, Santa Catherine's Day; I was too young to start work,
I had to be at least fourteen. So I changed the date on my working papers and
was hired as an assistant welder. I was also a mechanic for 25 years for some of the
most famous professional teams in the world's greatest races.

What is the best material for frame manufacturing (and why)?
Each period has had its own material. Today it is carbon fibre. We made bikes
from steel, then titanium, but titanium is too heavy – 15 per cent too heavy – then
aluminium and now carbon. So the next big material after carbon? I have no idea.

What is the most exciting new development in frame design or tubing technology?
The next one? I have made a lot of bicycles, but the most beautiful is the one that is
yet to come.

What's the most important element to the frame?
Every part of the frame is important.

What do you want to achieve for your customers?
I always try to give to my customer the best and we are careful to not disappoint
their expectations.

Who is/was the best frame manufacturer or builder and why?
No comment.

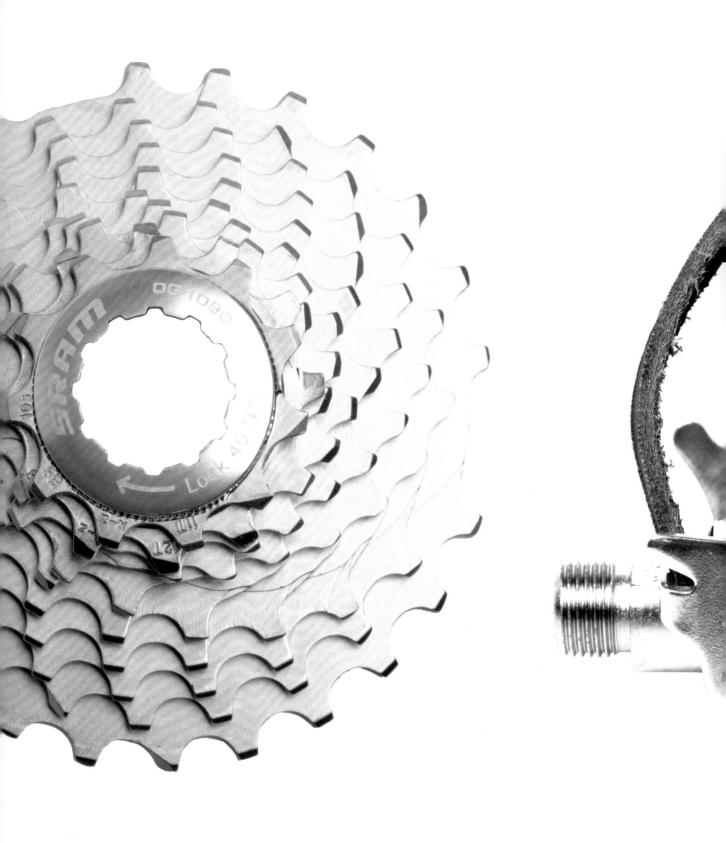

The Drive

Pedals

Before 1983 pedals had remained almost unchanged for decades. Campagnolo pattern quill pedals, combined with toe clips and leather straps, were widely recognized as the professional's choice and this design was copied by just about everyone. It was a bit of sideways thinking from Look, a French ski-binding company, that kick-started the pedal revolution for bicycles.

The clipless pedal

When Look examined the bicycle pedal they realized that ski boots and cycling shoes had much in common. They removed all the superfluous metal clips and leather straps and focused on the cleat as the method of retaining the shoe into the pedal. The resulting design was a 'step in and twist out' pedal, which is more or less what we have today. At around the same time Keywin in New Zealand also launched a new pedal. Lighter and better resolved than Look's original, the design owed much to Look's shoe plate pattern, but had a much simpler method for binding. However, Keywin were outmanoeuvred by Look, who had a much bigger marketing budget and the foresight to sponsor the La Vie Clare professional road team who, with Bernard Hinault, promptly won the Tour de France in 1985.

Campagnolo were the first big company with a decent marketing spend to react to Look's ingenious (now market-leading) pedal. They launched their ridiculously over-complicated and heavy SGR pedal in 1987. This system requires the cleat to slide into place and twist to exit. It couldn't compete with Look and was withdrawn soon afterwards. Campagnolo still make a clipless pedal, the Pro-Fit system, which is a cross between Look's cleat design and Time's binding spring mechanism. Although well made and effective they remain less popular than those produced by the more established manufacturers.

Some riders had knee injury issues with these early clipless pedals, especially when swapping over from standard pedals with toe clips and straps – the cleat had to be perfectly aligned, otherwise the foot could be held at an unfamiliar angle. Some riders believed that the standard clips and straps set-up allowed for better contact and alignment with the pedals. The clipless system was a sea change in pedalling technique, so it was unusual and it took time to get used to it.

In 1988 French company Time released their first clipless pedal, the TBT. It was the first clipless pedal to offer some rotational float to the foot, allowing the rider to have some freedom of

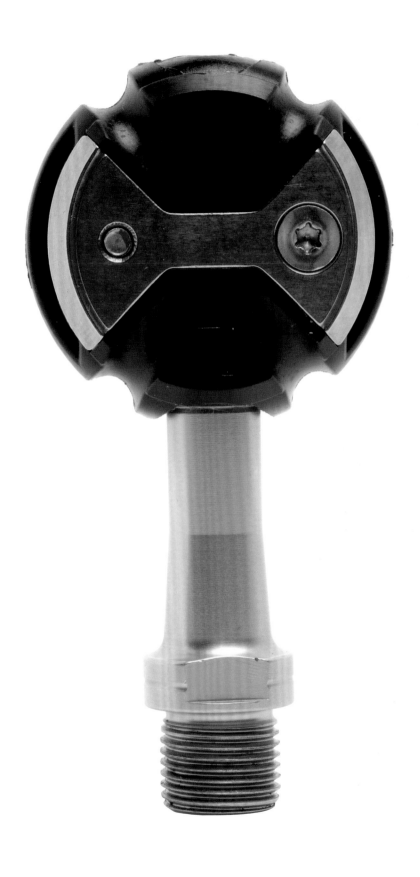

movement. It was heavy and complicated, but caught on with riders concerned about knee issues. In the late 1980s Mavic also took Look's cleat design to produce a pedal and, like Time, they added some free float. The result was a very large pedal that had a sliding mechanism built into the pedal platform. While it was clunky and made from dreadful materials, they had also addressed the issue of adjustable float. Look eventually took on the float issue by simply changing the shape of the cleat to allow some movement. This was crude but effective and allowed them to stick with their tried and tested retention system.

Look continued to dominate. Shimano were late to react to the road pedal market, as they had been occupied with the off-road clipless pedal and their Shimano Pedalling Dynamics (SPD – known in the mountain bike world as 'SPuDs') design. In 1988 Shimano took the direct route to the market by licensing the Look pattern pedal and adding their own, much improved, replaceable bearing system that had been developed for the SPuDs. Shimano's first in-house-designed clipless road pedal came in 1993. It was a scaled-down version of Look's design, using their two-hole SPD shoe cleat. There was some float in the pedal cleat when engaged but the result was pretty crude and the small cleat created problems with the contact surface area. Many riders found the system tricky to engage and with less support the cleat could sometimes rock on the pedal body, creating problems with foot stability. Eventually

Shimano went in search of their own patent and the result was the SPD-R system, which was a little too strong in spring release for road riders and, although still popular nowadays with track riders for its added security, they had to make a more useable road version.

Nowadays 'clipless' pedal choice is huge. Look still use the same three-bolt fixing cleat and it has changed little since the first white pedal hit the market. This is perhaps one of the only industry standard fixing methods and the reason why Look has remained marked leader for so long – most shoes use Look's three-bolt fixing holes. Additional float has been added and materials and manufacture have obviously improved, but it's a testament to how well the design was conceived that few have managed to better it. There are different systems but most have stuck to the step-in, twist-out pedal. There are many pedal systems available now, all promising better ergonomics, power transfer and cleat release, but as a rule professional riders will choose from the Look, Shimano, Time or Speedplay systems, as they make the most reliable and readily available pedals.

After several designs the latest and most successful incarnation of Shimano's clipless pedal is the SPD-SL. The Dura-Ace version of this system is favoured by many professional riders, including Lance Armstrong. It is very similar to Look's design and features an extra-wide platform and lightweight

Left to right Time, Mavic and Look Kéo clipless pedals

construction. The main advantage with Shimano's product line is that they have a pedal at various qualities and price points, all using the same cleat design.

The American pedal company Speedplay introduced a new idea to the clipless pedal arena. Before their intervention most mainstream pedals had the mechanism attached or incorporated into the pedal binding. Speedplay took the mechanism and integrated it into the pedal cleats. Their first pedal, the X pedal, allowed for almost free float, which took some getting used to but set a new benchmark for rotational float. This was done by using a circular pedal body, which looks a bit like a lollipop, with no moving parts and a simple spring retainer that was retained in a plastic shoe cleat. This meant that the pedal could be double-sided, which was safer and easier to locate onto and also that the weight could be reduced by a considerable amount. In addition, it moved the foot nearer the pedal axle and had unparalleled cornering clearance (up to 39°).

Speedplay's latest pedal, the Zero is, next to Look, one of the most popular pedal choices in the professional peloton. It allows for 15° of very fine float adjustment (or complete lock-out) and has improved spring tension for added security. Their light weight makes them very popular and they are around 100g (3½oz) lighter than their nearest competitor.

Speedplay X pedals are still being made, more than ten years after they were launched, which shows that they had it right first time around – most of their competitors have updated and reviewed their systems several times.

Time's latest system has remained true to its original free-floating design. Their RXS and XEN pedals both have a very low stack height (the distance between the sole of the foot and the pedal axle) and Q factor (see also Cranks, page 172). These features alone make it popular with many fastidious professional riders concerned about the fine tuning of their pedal set-ups. In addition to its technical advances Time's latest pedal, the RXS Ulteam Ti Carbon, features a hollow titanium axle and a carbon-reinforced composite body. Time also added titanium springs and aluminium bearing lockrings, which results in a more complicated pedal than Look's Kéo pedal, but matches it for weight at 180g (6¼oz).

Look have removed more and more material from their pedals over the years. Their Kéo system pedals have a similar cleat to the ones they started with but a minimal pedal mechanism. The Kéo fit system helps you choose the correct cleat – one that corresponds with the amount of float desired – up to 9° of rotation is available. The range-topping Kéo pedals weigh in at 180g (6¼oz) a pair and, 25 years on, Look still seem to be the most popular choice for pro riders.

Cassettes

In 1984 Shimano launched the first indexed Dura-Ace road groupset. The reception was mixed and it took a while to reach the discerning professional riders. But for racing bikes it meant that the days of poor shifting and bad freewheel gear ratios were numbered.

The improvements in the function of gear components have seen sprocket clusters grow from six indexed gears on the original Shimano indexed systems to 11 sprockets on the current Campagnolo Chorus, Record and Super Record groupsets. These developments have taken the once 10-speed racer to the current standard 20-speed (or up to 30 if you use a triple chainset) so now there are more than enough gear ratios for any racing situation. The main benefit with more cassette sprockets on the rear hub is that there are fewer 'missed' ratios and this gives the ability to stay in one front chainring longer. This is better because less time is spent shifting and readjusting derailleurs than previously.

Shimano and Campagnolo now use clusters of sprockets fused together in a few groups to make servicing and installation easier. However, this does mean that one worn sprocket in the cluster cannot be replaced without replacing the entire unit. Over the years the cassette sprockets have also changed in profile, adding ramps and cutaway teeth to assist the chain as it climbs up the gears. The result is a slick shift with minimal effort and less crunching of the gears. It does mean that gears have to be properly serviced and maintained and chains have to be replaced regularly to prevent wear to the sprocket teeth. If kept clean and maintained cassettes last well – changing the chain every 2,000k (1,242 miles) or so will keep the cassette running smoothly for several thousand kilometres.

SRAM's latest Red cassette goes one step further than the cluster system adopted by Shimano and Campagnolo. This is the biggest advance in cassette engineering for a while. The cassette is machined from one piece of material and is ingeniously located on the freehub body, with a simple cover plate behind the biggest sprocket. It is much lighter than Campagnolo's titanium Record cassette and will work (although not officially) with Shimano gears.

Campagnolo's 11-speed cassette offers riders a very smooth transition through the gears but the narrower chain and tighter tolerances versus 9- and 10-speed versions do require precise set-up and considered maintenance.

GEARING

Shimano standard ratios:

10-speed: 11–21 11–23 11–25 11–27 11–28 12–23 12–25 12–27

Campagnolo standard ratios:

10-speed: 11–21 11–23 11–25 12–23 12–25 13–26 13–29

11-speed: 11–25 12–25 12–27

SRAM standard ratios

10-speed: 11–23 11–25 11–26 11–28

To achieve alternative ratios with 10-speed gear components you will have to use either a Marchiso or a Mavic cassette. The big difference is that they use individual sprockets with spacers rather than the pre-made clusters of sprockets that Shimano, Campagnolo and SRAM use. They are less likely to shift as well as the cassettes from the main manufacturers as they aren't developed as a part of the complete gear system. However, they can make more wheels compatible with Shimano's or Campagnolo's different spacings, as the cassette-to-freehub adaptors can be chosen to suit the different gear mechanisms and shifters.

The Custom Road Bike

Chains

The bicycle roller chain design is unique. It is amazingly efficient and, as a result, has remained almost unchanged for decades. Nowadays ½in pitch chain has become the standard, although the quest for more and more gear sprockets has resulted in the thinning of the profile and some rather involved link engineering.

Chain companies have designed derailleur chains with obsolescence in mind, and they now wear out more quickly than ever. The thinner chains made for 10-speed gear systems use improved materials and these chains are very strong, but the nature of the gear shift, with repeated forcing of the gears into the bottom sprocket as the road tilts upwards, places side loads on the links that stretch the links and slowly wear the cassette sprockets. Hasty gear changes and poorly maintained chains and drivetrains result in a lot of worn-out chains.

The chain is made up of side plates (external links) and internal links with rollers inside them. The roller width defines the size of the chain – rollers on most derailleur-geared racing bikes are ³⁄₃₂in wide. The overall width of the chain determines whether it will fit the cassette sprockets. Campagnolo took the rivets and made them flush with the side plates, which makes the chain narrower but also makes it impossible to break with a roadside repair chain tool. They started at 6.1mm for their first 10-speed chain and now have reduced the width to a staggering 5.5mm, which makes you wonder what happens when the sprint winds up to 70kmh (43mph) and the riders push 53/11. Indeed, when 10-speed chains first arrived there were problems with installation (not material failures), and some infamous snapping incidents made for some very nervous team mechanics. Hence the installation instructions for all 10-speed chains are very involved.

Obviously a narrow chain isn't going to last forever – with an average life of around 3,000k (2,000 miles) they hardly last longer than the average set of racing tyres. Don't be fooled into thinking that thinner chains with hollow pins save a lot of weight either. At 245g, Campagnolo's Ultra Shift 11-speed chain is light, but it's only about 20g lighter than a 9-speed chain. While 9-speed chains can be fixed with a chain tool, 11-speed chains need a lot more care, so if you are planning a touring trip of the Himalayas, stick with something that you can fix.

Left Track chains are much stronger (and simpler) than the chains needed for derailleur systems. They do not need to shift between sprockets but they do have to withstand powerful sprints.

Links

The modern derailleur chain is now so thin and delicate it needs specialist tools to break it if you want to clean it thoroughly or repair it, should it fail when you are half-way up Alpe d'Huez.

The SRAM PowerLock link is a useful, 'no tools' solution to breaking and rejoining all their chains (one is available for 8-, 9- and 10-speed chains). They are compatible with all models of SRAM road chains. Wippermann make a similar link for speedy removal but the best of the current crop is Shimano's sliding 'puzzle' link on their Dura-Ace 7900 chain. Ingenious and simple to break, you can use it again and again (what were they thinking?). Campagnolo have yet to supply a 'no tools' link.

Compatibility

In my experience chains from different manufacturers are pretty, as long as the width of the chain is the right dimension (8-, 9- or 10-speed). I'm always surprised to see professional bikes using non-groupset chains on their bikes. Shimano seem to be the most popular choice for groupset deviants (even with Campagnolo-sponsored teams).

Track Chains

Why are track chains so chunky? The chains won't move from side to side, so they will last years rather than months. The chain is thick so that it stays in contact with the sprockets and cannot 'jump' off the chainwheel. The sprockets and chainwheels on all track bikes are designed to be used with an ⅛in chain, so ³⁄₃₂in chains won't work. Japanese track chains are best (Izumi, DID and HKK), although Wippermann's Whitestar chain is a favourite of mine and SRAM's (Sachs) PC7X nickel chain is really good value.

WIPPERMANN
Wippermann make a stainless-steel chain that doesn't cost the earth and works exceptionally well. Even after a long wet ride no rust spots will form. Their Connex 10-, 9- and 8-speed chains are simple and reliable and, with their Connex chainlink, very easy to install and service.

As chains have narrowed chain tools have needed greater levels of precision. Nowadays they are better quality to install chains accurately.

CAMPAGNOLO

Campagnolo pioneered the 10-speed chain and shifting system in 1999. The chain has been through several changes over the past few years and the result was the Ultra Narrow 10-speed chain and, latterly, the Ultra Shift 11-speed chain. This does require very careful installation as the pins and links are very delicate. If you must have 11 sprockets and you ride your bike a lot, you will need to invest in a very expensive chain tool and prepare for a big service bill too, as the chain will need to be changed around three to four times a year.

SRAM

SRAM's chain supplier started off life as Sachs/Sedis, two huge European chain manufacturers. Their expertise resulted in perhaps the best shifting and most reliable chains on the market. SRAM now own these companies and they have created the easiest to install 10-speed chain system to date. It is used in their Force and Rival Road race groupsets.

SHIMANO

Shimano changed the outside plate design to make shifting smooth and effortless. In their 8-speed chain they 'bulged' the side plates to assist the pick-up of the chain on the cassette sprockets and chainwheels. The usually conservative chain design has been up-ended by Shimano with the new asymmetric plate design of the Dura-Ace 10-speed 7900 chain. This shape is intended to improve the contact with the cogs, without sacrificing their trademark subtle shift. Other improvements to the links provide greater durability, with less noise – you can hardly hear a thing. Use of hollow pins drops the weight by only around 18g, but they do look very stylish, almost jewel-like. Shimano state that it only works with their 10-speed cassettes.

Dario Pegoretti

Via Brenta 46
38052 Caldonazzo
Trento
Italy
www.pegoretticicli.com

'Fatti con le mani'
'Made by hand'

Dario Pegoretti is one of the most influential bike builders around today. Once a good racer himself (no mean sprinter, if the reports are anything to go by), Pegoretti's skill was refined in the workshop of his father-in-law, Luigino Milani, in Ilasi, near Verona. Milani bikes were never big news, but Milani was certainly one of the leading frame builders of the 1970s and local racers favoured his skills. Eventually Dario would build the team bikes and follow the riders in training to 'watch his work in motion'. A bike fit, he says, is only truly realized in action. Here, he says, can you can see the rider's technique and pedalling style. Changes would be made, rebuilds carried out and self-confessed mistakes corrected – it was all essential experience for Pegoretti.

Pegoretti's big technical breakthrough was during the 1990s when he started experimenting with TIG welding steel tubing. He worked in close collaboration with Dedacciai, themselves a new and innovative company headed up by disgruntled Columbus workers. Columbus (and latterly Dedacciai) were the Italian arch rivals of the British tubing company Reynolds, and held a huge market share in Italy. For over a decade Pegoretti worked alongside many of the tubing manufacturers to design and develop new tubesets, notably Dedacciai but also French tube makers Excell. He was the first in Italy successfully to use TIG-welding techniques and the Dyna Lite and Radius tubesets that were the result of these efforts became the height of steel sophistication. Pegoretti was on to something.

So from 1991 to 1997, Pegoretti built frames almost exclusively for bike suppliers who also supported pro road teams, namely Pinarello and Carrera. Take a look under Miguel Indurain, Stephen Roche, Claudio Chiappucci *et al.* during that era and Dario's work is clearly identifiable – Indurain's extended head tube was (and still is) a Pegoretti signature detail.

Pegoretti found that his perfectly mitred and TIG welded tubes saved considerable weight over their lugged counterparts. Saving bike weight for the high mountain passes was something that the pros were asking for, but at a time when builders still preferred to build steel frames with lugs and when heat-treated alloys were still unreliable and uncomfortable it was hard to fulfill their desires. Pegoretti's technique was perfected and his approach influenced developments and huge technical advances in steel tubing – things he is still involved in today, most notably oversized formed steel sections. He still works on tubing technology, developing techniques for stainless-steel tubes and his own blend of Columbus tubing with US builder Richard Sachs (PegoRichie

tubes). With an artist's creativity and an engineer's skill he has applied techniques and craft to his work that few would attempt to emulate. Nowadays he still makes bold statements in his bicycle designs with fat tubes and an array of seat and chainstay profiles.

Bikes are an emotional topic for anyone involved in the sport and for Dario more than most. Cyclists make buying decisions based on what sparks that emotion. Interestingly, these days, very few Italians buy Pegoretti bikes, so most of the bikes go to the US and further afield.

But what sets Pegoretti bikes apart from the rest is that they are immaculately finished and ooze personality, all with personal attention from Dario. From tube selection to paint finishes and sometimes even with personal messages written on the bike by Dario – it all points to one thing: Pegoretti's are certainly made by hand and with love.

'So probably 10 per cent need a custom-built frame. But 100 per cent need a good fit.'

Materials used:
Steel and aluminium.

Employees:
3

Price range:
€1,900 to 3,000.

Waiting period (average!):
Eight months.

Frames built per year:
Around 350.

Who are your customers and how would you 'define' them?
Up to date, those who are looking for a classic ride on something different.

How long have you been building bikes?
35 years.

Do you make (or have you made) frames for any professional riders or teams?
Yes, many, in the past.

What started your interest in bicycle engineering/design?
Lack of money.

Who taught you to build?
Luigino Milani.

Who influences what you do now (if not all of the above)?
Nobody. There is a reason to build a frame in a certain shape, not just a question of following the market – not just for money. I think it is stupid just to follow the market… it is more fun to make the market, it's really hard of course… but for some reason I think it is correct.

'I was a little bit crazy, but I'd take the guys and take them to the workshop and hand them the torch and say "here you go".'

What is the best material for frame manufacturing (and why)?
Material is not the most important thing, there is not a 'best' material.
The choices in function of the material that you decide to use, experience
and craftsmanship are more important. You can find good and bad steel
frames out there, and also good and bad aluminium frames.

How do you size your customers?
With a measuring tape. Normally there is some customer that has an idea
and the other point is that 90 per cent of riders don't need a custom frame.
Because if you ask the rider, everyone has some problem with the back, with
the shoulder, everybody in the world… and if you ask the customer everybody
wants a 'comfortable' frame. So probably 10 per cent need a custom-built frame.
But 100 per cent need a good fit. In Europe there is a different culture about
cycling; there are a lot of older shops with plenty of sizing experience.

What is the most exciting new development in frame design or tubing technology?
Nothing very exciting. I think it is more important to have a good position and
learn to ride the bike correctly, than to have the latest carbon frame.

What's the most important element to the frame?
The design of the tubes and the experience of the builder, who has to be gifted.

What do you want to achieve for your customers?
Sometimes I try to convince the customers when they have made bad choices.
In the past it was more difficult because I remember when guys would come
to the shop and say I want this chainstay and this angle here and there. So
probably, I was a little bit crazy, but I'd take the guys and take them to the
workshop and hand them the torch and say 'here you go'. It's something like,
you have a problem with your body, do you go to your doctor and do you
speak with a surgeon and tell him what to do? It's a question of respect. I
say to my customers, when you ride a bike, when you start to ride a bike you
must think about the bike and yourself, and the machine. It's not about just
turning the pedals.

Who is/was the best frame manufacturer or builder and why?
I prefer to take an example from the past, Ugo de Rosa, because he could keep
the same high level of quality during the months and years joined with a good
production quantity.

Talking nowadays take a look at frame builder collective at www.framebuilders.org
and then add Mr Nagasawa.

Guide to Builders

STEEL
Independent Fabrication – www.ifbikes.com
Dario Pegoretti – www.pegoretticicli.com
Richard Sachs – www.richardsachs.com
Scapin – www.scapin.com
Tommasini – www.tommasini.com
Mercian – www.merciancycles.com
Vanilla – www.vanillabicycles.com
Gios – www.gios.it
De Rosa – www.derosanews.com
Ben Serotta – www.serotta.com

ALUMINIUM
Dario Pegoretti – www.pegoretticicli.com
De Rosa – www.derosanews.com
Storck – www.storck-bicycle.de
Gios – www.gios.it

TITANIUM
Merlin – www.merlinbike.com
Independent Fabrication – www.ifbikes.com
Ben Serotta – www.serotta.com
De Rosa – www.derosanews.com
Seven Cycles – www.sevencycles.com
Moots – www.moots.com
Lynskey – www.lynskeyperformance.com
Titus – www.titusti.com

CARBON FIBRE
Independent Fabrication – www.ifbikes.com
Ben Serotta – www.serotta.com
Crumpton – www.crumptoncycles.com
Parlee – www.merciancycles.com
Colnago – www.colnago.com
Cyfac – www.cyfac.fr
De Rosa – www.derosanews.com
Calfee – www.calfeedesign.com
Kestrel – www.kestrelbicycles.com
Storck – www.storck-bicycle.de
Aegis – www.aegisbicycles.com

This list is by no means exhaustive, these are some of the builders that I have experience of. I have ridden their bikes and think that they do a good job; in some cases they do a very good job.

Sad to say Italian and British frame building isn't what it once was, so many of these builders are American and this is a direct result of the growth of the frame building industry in the US. Some say this is because the US customer is more discerning, some say that it is because the level of skill and materials technology is highest there. Either way they all take a similar approach and all good builders will devote considerable time and care to making your dream bike a reality.

But don't just take my word for it. Finding a great bike takes time and you will need to listen to a lot of opinion and advice from riding friends, bike shop sales staff and local bike builders. Above all, though, always ask people what bike they ride and why. The answers will tell you far more than I can do in this book.

So, here are some of the builders that still do custom bikes, still believe in handmade frames and still spend time with the customer to get exactly what they want. As I said, it's not exhaustive, but this list will get you going in the right direction.

But whatever bike you end up with remember to enjoy your search and enjoy the ride.

Websites and Further Reading

WEBSITES:

www.handmadebicycleshow.com
If you want to take a peek at the latest handmade frames available, try a visit to the North American Handmade Bike Show.

www.fixedwheel.co.uk
Try this site to work out your gear ratios. There's a useful mph table too and they also have plenty of valuable information and advice.

www.hubjub.co.uk
Excellent shopping site for fixed wheel and track bikes.

www.bicyclebearing.com
Need a cartridge bearing for your bike? This is the place to look.

www.weightweenies.starbike.com
Useful resource for those obsessed with weight.

www.framebuilders.org
A collective of powerful frame-building brains, including Richard Sachs and Dario Pegoretti.

www.dtswiss.com
Excellent spoke-length calculator and wheel-weight approximator.

www.competitivecyclist.com
A shopping site full of great products, useful information and sound advice.

www.sapim.be
Makers of spokes for many of the wheelsets made by Rolf, Zipp etc.

www.campagnolo.com
A lot more than just a product website.

www.frameforum.org
A great forum for the discussion of frame building and the like.

www.velo-retro.com
Useful resource for collectors and enthusiasts.

www.campyonly.com
Everything you need to know about Campagnolo.

www.cyclocrossworld.com
A shopping site that offers plenty of top cyclo-cross products and advice for racers.

www.serottacyclinginstitute.com
If you want to find a fitting expert, these guys train them.

www.sheldonbrown.com
The best resource on the web for anything, compatibility-wise or mechanical, related to bicycles.

www.velobase.com
Want to know about a component? And see a picture? Here's the place (be warned – you'll lose a few hours on it…).

www.retrobike.co.uk
Mostly mountain bikes but features a great auction search engine.

www.pezcyclingnews.com
One of the better bike review sites.

www.uci.ch
For bicycle regulations and machine technical specifications for racing.

www.disraeligears.co.uk
An incredible collection of derailleur gears with pictures and technical information.

www.speedplay.com
Very good pedals and a great pedal history page.

www.thehortoncollection.com
Memorabilia and the like, an amazing collection.

www.memoire-du-cyclisme.net
Huge archive for race results and team information (in French).

www.shimano.com
Everything you need to know about the Japanese components.

www.classicrendezvous.com
Loads of pictures and up-to-date information about retro and classic components.

BOOKS:

Barnett, John
Barnett's Manual: Analysis and Procedure for Bicycle Mechanics
(Boulder, CO: VeloPress, rev. 5th ed., 2003).
The guide for professional workshops.

Berto, Frank J., Raymond Henry and Robert Shepherd
The Dancing Chain: History and Development of the Derailleur Bicycle
(San Francisco, CA: Van Der Plas Publications, 3rd ed., 2008).
Has as many fans as critics, but the content on the history of the derailleur is vast.

Borysewicz , Eddie
Bicycle Road Racing: Complete Program for Training and Competition
(Vermont: Vitesse Press, 1988).
Takes a while to digest but it's essential reading if you are into bike racing.

Bouvet, Philippe, Pierre Callewaert, Jean-Luc Gatellier and Serge Laget, trans. David Herlihy
Paris-Roubaix: A Journey Through Hell (Boulder, CO: VeloPress, 2007).
The hardest race on bikes and riders, a good guide to the world's toughest bike race.

Brandt, Jobst
The Bicycle Wheel (Pearl River, NY: Avocet Press, 3rd ed., 1993).
The bible for wheel builders and a guide to starting out on building your own wheels.

Burke, Edmund R. and Chris Carmichael
Serious Cycling (Pudsey, West Yorkshire: Human Kinetics Europe, rev. 2nd ed., 2002).
If you want to get fitter and faster look no further.

Burrows, Mike
Bicycle Design: The Search for the Perfect Machine (London: Snowbooks, 2008).
Plenty of background on bicycle science.

De la Rosa, Denise M. and Michael J. Kolin
The Custom Bicycle: Buying, Setting Up and Riding the Quality Bicycle
(London: Thorsons, 1985).
This book may be 30 years old but is almost truer now than it was then.

Doughty, Simon
The Long Distance Cyclists' Handbook (Guilford, CT: Lyons Press, 2nd ed., 2006).
The best book there is on long distance riding.

Facchinetti, Paolo and Guido Rubino
Campagnolo: 75 Years of Cycling Passion (Boulder, CO: VeloPress, 2008).
Lots of history and pictures of Campagnolo.

Herlihy, David
Bicycle: The History (London: Yale University Press, 2004).
Quirky coffee table book.

Paterek, Tim
The Paterek Manual For Bicycle Framebuilders
(California: Henry James, 3rd ed., 2004).
This book is full of information – if you are considering having
a go at building a bike, you will definitely want to read it.

Perry, David B.
Bike Cult: The Ultimate Guide to Human-Powered Vehicles
(New York, NY: Four Walls Eight Windows, 1995).
Sociology meets cycling.

Schraner, Gerd
The Art of Wheelbuilding: A Bench Reference for Neophytes, Pros & Wheelaholics
(Ann Arbor, MI: Ann Arbor Press, 1999).
He taught me to build a wheel and worked the six-day race scene for decades.

Snowling, Steve and Ken Evans
Bicycle Mechanics: In Workshop and Competition
(Pudsey, West Yorkshire: Human Kinetics Europe, 1987).
A classic reference book for professional bike mechanics.

Van Der Plas, Rob
Cycle History (Minneapolis, MN: Motorbooks International, 1988).
A good and insightful guide to cycle history.

Van Der Plas, Rob
**Bicycle Technology: Understanding, Selecting and
Maintaining the Modern Bicycle and its Components**
(Mill Valley, CA: Bicycle Books, 1990).
A bit dated but provides plenty of sound advice from a experienced mechanic.

Wilson, David Gordon
Bicycling Science (Cambridge, MA: MIT Press, rev. 2nd ed., 2004).
A text book read that has plenty of explanation of the physics of cycling.

Woodland, Les
Cycle Racing: Training To Win (London: Pelham Books, rev. 2nd ed., 1988).
The best book I have read on coaching and bicycle racing.

Zinn, Lennard
Zinn and the Art of Road Bike Maintenance
(Boulder, CO: VeloPress, rev. 2nd ed., 2005). The classic on how to fix your bike.

JUST FOR INSPIRATION:

Augendre, Jacques
Fausto Coppi (Ottershaw, Surrey: Bromley Books, 2000).
The classiest rider ever, with plenty of wonderful images.

Bobet, Jean, trans. Adam Berry
Tomorrow we ride (Norwich, Norfolk: Mousehold Press, 2008).
Why we ride and why we love bikes, explained by an ex-pro, who can write too.

Brunel, Philippe
An Intimate Portrait of the Tour De France: Masters and Slaves of the Road
(Denver, CO: Buonpane Publications, 2nd ed., 1977).
The stars who were created at the world's biggest bike race. Beautifully photographed.

Fournel, Paul, trans. Allan Stockel
Need for the Bike (Nebraska: University of Nebraska Press, 2003).
A book of essays about the beauty and pleasure of riding a bike.

Krabbe, Tim, trans. Sam Garrett
The Rider (London: Bloomsbury Publishing, 2002).
The author of *The Vanishing* approaches a cycle race with the same intrigue.

Seaton, Matt
The Escape Artist: Life from the Saddle (London: Fourth Estate, 2002).
Real life and how the addiction to our sport weaves through it. A wonderful book.

Strickland, Bill
Ten Points (New York, NY: Hyperion Books, 2007).
Inspirational and very heartfelt biography of a writer and racer.

Acknowledgements

My personal thanks go to the photographers Gerard Brown, Ben Ingham and Camille J McMillan. Also to Jonathan Bacon for his attention to every detail and to *Rouleur* magazine, especially the contributors who have inspired and helped with this book – Kadir Guirey and Rohan Dubash. I owe a huge debt of gratitude to Jo Lightfoot and Donald Dinwiddie at Laurence King Publishing, who were very patient and determined to make this book happen. And lastly, to Taz and Gino.

Special thanks to all the manufacturers and suppliers who have helped with this book:

Condor Cycles – Grant Young, Greg Needham, Neil Manning and all the guys at Grays Inn Road are always there to fix a last-minute problem and I am very grateful.

Shimano – Harald Troost
SRAM – Gaetan Vetois
Campagnolo – Thanks to Tulio, the man who started it all
Lightweight wheels – Paul Bolwell at Wiggle
Mavic – Michel Lethenet
Royce Engineering – Cliff Polton
Pauls Components – Paul
Phil Wood – Darla Sasaki
Chris King – Chris DiStefano
Joe Ingram and the team at Independent Fabrication
Richard Sachs
Ernesto Colnago
Dario Pegoretti
Parlee – Tom Rodi and Bob Parlee
Ben Serotta and Phil Cavell
Continental tyres – Shelley Childs
Fizik saddles – Jamie Newall
Edge Composites – Jason Sager
Brooks saddles – Andrea Menenghelli
And also to the UK distributors and suppliers:
Madison Cycles – Albert Steward for San Marco, DT, Shimano, PRO, Elite
          and a bunch of other stuff
Upgrade bikes – Dom Mason and Tom Marchment for TRP and other stuff
Windwave – Peter Nisbet for Nokon cables and Colnago
Chicken and sons – Mike Catlin and Cedric Chicken for TA, Time, Cinelli
          and Campagnolo
Sideways Cycles – Tim Johnson for White Industries

Guy Andrews

Index

'Life is like riding a bicycle. To keep your balance you must keep moving'

ALBERT EINSTEIN